Words of Praise
for
MEETING THE MASTER
IN THE GARDEN

William Griffin's translations are spiritual in the best sense of the word: they blow the dust off devotional classics by breathing fresh air into lively English paraphrases. Like his masters, Griffin knows that the Christian pilgrimage is serious play, a strange but exhilarating *pas de deux* between sacred and profane, a reverence for holy things and the joyful irreverence that only true holiness can inspire.

— GREGORY WOLFE, Writer in Residence and Director of the MFA Program, Seattle Pacific University; Publisher and Editor of *Image: A Journal of Arts & Religion*

Refracted through William Griffin's rollicking translation and commentary, these "lost" works of Thomas à Kempis come to new life. Who says spiritual wisdom has to be dull?

— ROBERT ELLSBERG, author of *All Saints: Daily Reflections* and *Saints' Guide to Happiness*

Griffin's helpful asides, scattered throughout the text, as well as in the afterword, provide illuminating background for someone wanting to go even deeper in reclaiming the old but far-from-musty insights of Kempis. A delight to read and ponder!

— TIMOTHY JONES, Episcopal priest and author of *The Art of Prayer*

The introduction was superb, and the inserts I found especially helpful; they are themselves a small compendium of wisdom for us today. What a clever way to make Kempis's words relevant for the modern reader! Midrash will never grow old as a way of opening up a text.

— MURRAY BODO, OFM, Franciscan priest, retreat-giver, poet, author of *Poetry as Prayer: Denise Levertov*

With Griffin, not only do inaccessible Christian classics become extraordinarily readable and personal, but we discover how much our own age has to learn from the past in terms of wisdom, devotion, and practicality.

— LUCI SHAW, poet, author, *The Crime of Living Cautiously*;
Writer in Residence, Regent College

Griffin's [translations] are books you can actually use as devotionals. Take them into your prayer closet and read them as they were meant to be read, slowly, a chapter or two at a time, as you think and pray about your life in God. You won't be hearing the distant and thus irrelevant voice of a remote and impossibly pious saint. Through Griffin's brilliant recoveries of the originals, you are going to hear a wise and intimate voice speaking to you in shockingly contemporary and sprightly terms about ultimate things — things you know in your heart.

— HAROLD FICKETT, novelist and essayist; author of
The Living Christ: The Extraordinary Lives of Today's Heroes

This is the first new English translation of Thomas à Kempis's *Garden of Roses* and *Valley of Lilies* in four hundred years, and it is enchanting. The instruction and inspiration of the author of the perennially popular *Imitation of Christ* have been rendered into language that is fresh, lively, and perfectly suited to Thomas's aphoristic style.

— FISHER HUMPHREYS, Beeson Divinity School, Samford University

MEETING THE MASTER
IN THE GARDEN

Translations of the Latin Spiritual Classics
By WILLIAM GRIFFIN

THOMAS À KEMPIS: THE IMITATION OF CHRIST
A Modern Version
2000

AUGUSTINE OF HIPPO: SERMONS TO THE PEOPLE
Advent, Christmas, New Year's, Epiphany
A Modern Version
2002

THOMAS À KEMPIS: CONSOLATIONS FOR MY SOUL
being a modern version of
SOLILOQUY OF THE SOUL
2003

AUGUSTINE OF HIPPO: HIGH ANXIETY
A Brief Life in His Own Words
2006

Thomas à Kempis
Author of *The Imitation of Christ*

MEETING THE MASTER IN THE GARDEN

How Jesus Cultivates Our Soul

being a translation of
Hortulus Rosarum (Garden of Roses)
&
Vallis Liliorum (Valley of Lilies)

A Contemporary Translation by
William Griffin

A Crossroad Book
The Crossroad Publishing Company
New York

The Crossroad Publishing Company
16 Penn Plaza – 481 Eighth Avenue, Suite 1550
New York, NY 10001

Printed in the United States of America

The text of this book is set in 11/14 Caslon and 10/14 Calligraphic 421. The display face is Prose Antique.

Cataloging-in-Publication Data is available from the Library of Congress.

ISBN 0-8245-2140-4

1   2   3   4   5   6   7   8   9   10   10   09   08   07   06   05

For MARGARET and JUSTIN CAMPBELL

Contents

Valley of Lilies

Afterword

Foreword

The Divine has done some of his finest work in gardens. First, in the garden of Eden, where he introduced Adam to Eve, she introduced him to fruit, and they introduced the rest of us to sin. Then, in Gethsemane, where Jesus came to grips with what the Father demanded of him. Finally, in the garden of Joseph of Arimathea, which included among other things the tomb he lent to Mary for her dead son; and was that the gardener Mary Magdalen got a brief glimpse of?

Thomas à Kempis has done some of his best spiritual writing in this book, *Meeting the Master in the Garden.* It's the overarching title for two of his works, *Garden of Roses* (*Hortulus Rosarum*) and *Valley of Lilies* (*Vallis Liliorum*).

Kempis was the fifteenth-century spiritual writer happily remembered for his master work, *The Imitation of Christ.* After the Bible it's thought to be the world's most widely read Christian book. He was born, lived, and died in the territory now known as the Netherlands. At an early age he entered a new group called the Brothers of the Common Life, and later joined an old group, the Canon Regulars of the Order of St. Augustine, in a new monastery dedicated to St. Agnes. For more about his life, please find "Who Was Kempis?" and "Who Owns Kempis?" below (pages 237–240).

Altogether he put together four anthologies: *Imitation of Christ,* published by HarperSanFrancisco in 2000, *Consolation for My Soul* (original title, *Soliloquy of a Soul*), recently published by Crossroad, and *Garden of Roses* and *Valley of*

Lilies, now published by Crossroad. All but the first appear in English translation for the first time in the last four hundred years.

How did Kempis pull it off? He himself explained it in "Mottos for Monks," where he invented a conversation between a visitor and himself (1).

"My dear monk, what do you do in your cell?"

"I read, and I write, and I collect honeys."

"Honeys?"

"Yes, and I hive the honeyed sayings — wisdom sayings, as it were — into little collections of my own."

Yes, Kempis's writings are collections, anthologies of the spiritual and secular wisdom that had passed across his writing desk over a period of sixty years. Each book has a general title. Each chapter of each book has a specific title.

The text in each chapter is really a bundle or boodle of maxims, emblems, adages, saws. No paragraphs of any significance, just sayings. Sort of like Ecclesiastes and Ecclesiasticus, Job and James, Proverbs and any number of sentences from the Psalms.

All of his books deal with virtues, the sort of virtues that would-be priests and nuns would need to survive as Augustinians; and that we moderns, religious or otherwise, need to survive as Christians.

Knowing all this, one doesn't just read a Kempis book from cover to cover. Open the book, yes, then pick a chapter, any chapter, and pray over it and through it. Read a sentence or a paragraph, pause, reflect, then say something to God if God hasn't already started speaking to your soul.

Remember, Kempis's works aren't like works of fiction with rising action, climax, falling action; nor are they well-argued works of nonfiction; nor are they multistep programs or sequences that last for forty days. What's the operative principle? Do one virtuous act, and you improve your whole spiritual life; fall victim to one vice, and you lower your whole spiritual life. Hence, one can begin anywhere.

Kempis's works are inspirational as well as instructional. They're wisdom books containing philosophical, theological, commonsensical insights. Pray through each of his books, and you will have completed the doctoral course, *Spirituality of the West*. They were originally aimed at a monastic audience of the fifteenth century, of course, but the reader can easily make the necessary adaptations for the twenty-first century audience, clerical as well as laical.

So why *Roses* and *Lilies*? Kempis gave us some clues.

"The person who has built his or her spiritual life on praying and meditating on celestial things joins the ranks of the Master Gardener, planting roses and lilies in his field" (*Roses*, 4).

And again.

"When you're in the garden or the orchard, count the different species and number the different trees; smell the flowers, especially the roses; taste the fruits, especially the pears; pinch the herbs, especially the thyme; and get a whiff of the lilies" (*Roses*, 19).

The translator of Latin spiritual classics into English today has two choices, literal translation or paraphrasal translation. The former would appear more faithful to the Latin text, but the resulting translation doesn't appear all that faithful to modern idiom. Paraphrasal translation, on the other hand, is more faithful to the original meaning by using contemporary English idiom. Older readers lean on the literal; younger readers prefer the paraphrasal; both methods are far from perfect. All of my translations — *Imitation* and *Consolations* as well as *Roses* and *Lilies* — are paraphrasal. Classic wisdom for the young and prayerful! For more on this subject, please see below "Translation, Literal or Paraphrasal" (page 247).

Information of historical and spiritual interest — perhaps more than the reader wants to know — will occasionally be found throughout the book. If and when the translation becomes tedious, the reader may want to move on to a helpful essay. "Another Way of Copying the Bible," "Jesus in the Garden," "A Seasoning for All Seasons," "Thoroughly Modern Clinging." For a complete list please see the table of contents; the essay titles are found in italics.

A final word. All translations are destined to fail, even this one. That's to say, they fall far short of the originals. Hence, the reader should make every effort to read the Latin originals, even if it means taking up Latin as a second or third language. The difficulties in doing so have been vastly overrated.

Even Cato the Elder (234–149 B.C.) took up the study of Greek when he was eighty. Of course, he had an advantage over the modern English reader; Greek was a sister language to Latin, sharing a common grammar and much the same vocabulary.

In no case should this paraphrasal translation be quoted or cited in scholarly work on Kempis. Only if the reader truly wants to know what Kempis actually meant should he or she turn to the next page.

Garden
of Roses

1

Clinging

*When you spend time with a convert, something of
the new enthusiasm rubs off. But when you spend time
with a pervert — that's to say, with someone who has
quite a different worldview from your own —
doesn't some of that rub off too?*

(Psalm VUL 17:26–27; NRSV 18:26–27)

Pay close attention to what I have to say, my dear devout.
Don't get dragged under the bushes by the salacious or men-
dacious. That'd be such a disgrace! Rather make friends with a
virtuous devout. A person of some edification and education.
Someone whose conversation tends to encourage you, not dis-
courage you. Indeed someone whose conversational style you
could well take up as your own.

Have you noticed how cold charcoal, when it hits hot coals,
spits heat itself? The same thing happens when a tepid devout
hangs with an ardent devout; that's to say, the lukewarm spirituality will begin to heat up. I've seen the same thing happen
when a fervent yet uneducated devout associates with a person of good intellectual and moral character. Improvement all
around.

What I'm talking about here is *clinging*. Not the sticky glue-paper kind, but the strong-fingered, rescue-at-the-edge-of-the-precipice sort of grasp. There are a hundred examples I could cite, some recent, some not so recent.

The apostles *clinging* to Christ till they were filled with the Holy Spirit.

Marcus *clinging* to Peter; the result was that he drank in the holy gospel, which he heard from the huge, joyful lips of Peter.

Timothy *clinging* to Paul; right from the beginning of his intellectual life, he mastered the Scriptures, as Paul noted in his second to Timothy (3:15); the further and indeed graceful result was his ordination as bishop in Ephesus; much loved by Paul as though he were the only son of a very loving father.

Polycarp *clinging* to the holy apostle John; he became a fervent and popular preacher of the faith and a willing martyr with Ignatius of Antioch.

Augustine *clinging* to Ambrose bishop of Milan; he became a glorious doctor of Holy Church, a title illustriously conferred by the whole world, and of course our most blessed founder and father.

Maurus *clinging* to Benedict; with God's help the young man eventually became an abbot himself with a saintly reputation for virtues and miracles.

Bernard *clinging* to the venerable abbot Stephen in the Cistercian monastery; a young beloved of God who became the light of religion in his own order.

So, what's so good about *clinging* to others?

Well, good friends help the health of a soul; bad friends don't. Good reading is helpful; trash talk isn't. Solitude with silence is helpful; hurly-burly isn't.

So, what's the obvious conclusion?

Spend some time with God, or just pal around with another devout, chatting about the virtues of Christ.

A terrible trap, spending your time only on intellectual curiosities. Study books if you must, but don't fail to investigate your vices — that will eat up your leisure time. As for what ails you intellectually and spiritually, apply only the time-honored remedies.

THOROUGHLY MODERN CLINGING

Clinging as a spiritual activity was popular with the writers of the Old and New Testaments as well as with such later spiritual masters as Augustine and Kempis, but few modern writers would think clinging a fit activity for anything but a parasitical vine.

The one exception seems to be Emilie Griffin. Her book, *Clinging: The Experience of Prayer,* originally published in 1983, has become something of an underground classic. For her, clinging is a wildly successful, if extremely dependent, plant.

"We must cling to the one reality that does not crumple, the one rock that will not be washed loose in the tide and onslaught of anything.

"We must cling to the one reality that will hold firm, though the earth be destroyed and the mountains flung into the sea and the sun put out.

"We must cling to the one who holds eternity in his hand, who will not perish in the end, and who has the power to save us, too; the one who knew us before we existed, in whose thought and by whose hand we exist from moment to moment.

"He chose and shaped us from our mother's womb to be intimate with him. This intimacy is what we were made for. Away from it, we feel at odds with existence and even with ourselves. Close to him, we are at peace. This is the one intimacy of which we need not be afraid, for it will not disappoint or betray us.

"On God we can loose all the intensity of what we are, all the passion and the longing we feel. This is the one surrender we can make in utter trust, knowing that we can rest our whole weight there and nothing will give away" (*Clinging,* third edition [Wichita: Eighth Day Press, 2003], 56).

This sounds like Kempis, and yet when the author wrote *Clinging* she had yet to read his *Imitation of Christ.*

"Clinging! That is the ecstasy the saints have told about. What they didn't always tell us was that it was so close by, as simple as turning one's face to the Lord instead of to the wall. What they did not fully describe to us was how suddenly the Spirit of God can be present, whenever, by an act of the will, we put ourselves into his company. It can happen in a moment, any moment. And when we have time for it, and the moments stretch out into an ocean of time, there is the chance, always, that our clinging will carry us along so far it feels as if there will be no returning" (61). — W.G.

2

Listening

***Just by listening,
the wise person becomes wiser still.***

(Proverbs 1:5)

Otherworldly wisdom — listen to its words, my new devout. In it you'll find more than all the wiseacres of the world can cough up.

Listen to the words of St. John in his first, for example, and you'll learn that it's not the world and the things in this world you should love (2:15). Hence, drain yourself of all your worldly poisons; open every spigot; unplug every orifice.

Listen to the words about the end without end, and temptation will fade away.

Beware of dangers to your soul.

Never commit a scandalous act.

Never say an indecent word.

Never let a relative come between you and God. If your earthly father gets in the way, tell him you have a heavenly Father to answer to. If your mother or sister tries to get a word in edgewise, speak to them just as directly.

Never tell a lie.

Of course, commend all your friends and relatives to God. Pray that they emend their lives. They should stay away from sins lest they offend God and lose all their celestial capital for mere terrestrial gains.

Some random bits of wisdom worth listening to.

We're mere mortals and, as such, we're subject to lies, telling them to others and believing the ones told to us.

Listen to what the wisdom of the other world has to say about the wisdom of this world.

If there's a party going on in your heart, it's due to the continuous stream of guests, invited and uninvited.

The world with its concupiscence won't last forever, according to John in his first (2:17). Its time will come, and so will mine, and so will my friends' and relatives' time.

Everything in this world is vanity. That's to say, honor, wealth, and power are hollow gourds, and we're the beans bouncing around inside. So why does the world have this attraction about it when there's nothing on it or in it that's clean, neat, elegant? The only decent activity is to do God and do good. And you can't do these until you condemn the world and all of its pomps.

Listen to what the wisdom of the other world has to say about the devil.

The devil has strewn the playing field of the Lord with hideous traps of all kinds and sizes, each with the power to maim or kill.

Most dangerous trap of all, and the one we all seem prey to with every step we take? Wealth. We want to be regarded as rich, honorable, powerful. At least according to Paul's first to Timothy (6:9).

The smaller traps can be just as destructive. Food and drink. A wandering eye. Mindless conversation. An unfaithful heart. The sheer tedium of trying to do good.

Everything's a trap, a trick, but to love God and do good — there's nothing tricky about that. But you can't love God perfectly until you downgrade yourself and the world. Do that, and God will reward you a hundred times over in the present, and that doesn't include what's to come; at least according to Jesus as recorded by Matthew (19:29).

Listen to the wisdom about death.

On this earth, my dear devout, you're only a wanderer, an exile, a pilgrim.

Death has distanced you from your relatives and your friends. Where are all those companions of yours? The ones who used to laugh and play with you? The person who visited you yesterday? That pleasant dinner companion of yours last night? Well, they're not here today. Vanished into thin air. Perhaps they're lying in a doorway somewhere dead as a doornail.

Some final wisdom about the world.

Woe to all those who are intoxicated with the world and all of its diversions! They're the sort of people whom every good society with any sense of joy in it doesn't associate with much while they're alive but does take the trouble to bury them when they're dead.

Well, they're dead and gone, most of them, passed the point of no return. Once, they were guests on earth, and so am I. Everything they had, they left behind, and so will I. They passed by here like shadows on a wall, and so will I.

By listening to the wisdom of the other world, my dear new devout, you'll grow wiser by the day.

∽∿∽∿∽∿∽∿

NEW TO MONASTICISM

"Otherworldly wisdom — listen to its words, my new devout." In this, the first sentence of the present chapter, Kempis tells us just who his audience was. New devouts; that's to say, men new to the spiritual life and religious life; men who wanted to become monks.

Which is to say, dear reader, that you may be as ignorant of monastic spirituality as the men and women who showed up at Augustine's or Benedict's doorstep looking for a better spiritual life. You'll find what they found, two preordained stages before one can become a monk or a nun. What have the two great monastic rules to say about this?

The Rule of St. Augustine, at least in its written form, isn't a rule at all and has nothing to say about new members. Such prescriptions and practices developed by the bishop of Hippo and his friends who gathered to enjoy the fruits of community living according to the gospels first appeared in a letter of his (211), dated A.D. 423; in it he addressed a nervous nun in Hippo who'd just been elected superior of her convent. Augustine's sister was once the superior there, a cousin and niece of his lived there, and most probably his former common-law wife and mother of his son, Adeodatus.

Here's what the Rule of St. Benedict, dating from 530 or thereabouts, has to say about newcomers.

"The monastery door shouldn't be opened to just anybody who comes a-calling. If that person truly wants to become a monk, he'll come again, and thump and thwack the door until he's let in. Put him up in the guest house. Once in, he must patiently endure whatever obstacles and difficulties the monks may put in his path. Four or five days of this, and if he hasn't already fled to the hills, then honor his request and invite him into the monastery.

"After that, invite him to join the novices and put him on their order of the day, studying, praying, meditating, eating, sleeping. A senior person or the master of novices should be put in charge of him, someone who knows how to win a soul.

"This same person should carefully determine whether the vocation to the monastery is real and the postulant is ready for the work of God; that's to say, for all sorts of obedience trials. The novice master should make it quite clear that the way to God is ragged as well as rugged" (51:1–8).

Which is another way of saying, dear reader, that you are the postulant, you are the novice, when it comes to the spirituality in this book. Read well, the rough as well as the smooth, and you'll hear the voice of a spiritual master, Thomas à Kempis, speaking not only to the new devouts in the fifteenth century but also to you in the twenty-first. — W.G.

3

Seeking

Find wisdom,
and you'll be a very happy person indeed.
(Proverbs 3:13)

Seek true wisdom. That's what Jesus taught; and he taught it by word and example.

The truly wise devout hates wickedness, speaks truth, and works justice.

The devout who lives soberly, seriously, chastely, piously, humbly, devoutly, and manages to sidestep the puddles of temptation is a wise person and pleasing to God.

Such a devout enjoys a good reputation. He keeps a good conscience. He leaves sadness behind. He possesses peace, and he frequently receives from God a heart full of joy.

All these the world has no knowledge of and hence no wisdom about.

Such wisdom as the world has is vanity. Looked at in God's lexicon, it's just another word for "stupidity." It deceives its own proponents and in the end disappoints its own adherents.

Death only promises to strangle the soul, according to Paul in his to the Romans (8:6). And death does come, suddenly and swiftly, carrying off the bibbers of wine and suckers of sweets. Now grief and pain. After the joys of the flesh, nothing but filth.

True wisdom, however, is drawn from the hidden words and sacred acts of Christ. His recommendation, sweetly and gently uttered, is to spurn the world, flee the bright lights, subjugate the flesh, endure the pain, undergo the rigors. And, oh yes, to love the virtues.

∽∾∽∾∽∾∽∾∽

WHEN KEMPIS WAS NEW TO MONASTICISM

From his earliest years Kempis wanted to be a monk. When the Monastery of St. Agnes was formed, he and two others were invited to join. Then in the presence of the whole monastic community, the three postulants — for that's what persons requesting permission to enter were called — prostrated themselves at the foot of the prior (who happened to be his older brother, John).

"What do you seek?" asked the prior, beginning the ritual for postulants.

"God's mercy and your own good company," replied the three.

The prior then bade them rise from their prostrate position, but stay on their knees. Then the monks felt free to pepper the aspirants with questions about worldly obligations and canonical impediments. These inquiries having been satisfactorily answered, the prior proceeded to point out to them the gravity of the step they contemplated, the hardships of the life, and the severe punishments inflicted on those who failed in the strict observance of their obligations.

"Do you still persevere in your request?" asked the prior.

"We trust by the grace of God and the aid of the prayers of the community to fulfill all the duties that you have laid before us."

"God grant that you may fulfill them all and thereby gain eternal life." Then the prior took the hands of each of the postulants, a sign of his giving them the run of the monastery. "In the name of God and in our own name we receive you and grant you our fellowship."

The date of their receiving the religious habit was then announced, the feast of Corpus Christi, a relatively new devotion, and the postulants withdrew. They prepared for their reception by a thorough examination of conscience and a general confession of the sins of their lives.

On the day itself, he and his companions went to the monastery sacristy after the hour of tierce had been chanted (between nine and noon). There they were divested of their secular clothes and invested in the habit of the order. A white cassock or soutane and over that a plain linen surplice or garment, ranging from knee-length to ankle-length, which, to signify that they had yet to bind themselves with vows of religion, had no sleeves.

All processed to the sanctuary. The canons knelt in their stalls. The prior, assisted by deacon and subdeacon, knelt before the altar. The three postulants lay prostrate on the floor. A hymn to the Holy Spirit was intoned (*Veni Creator Spiritus*). The prior chanted the versicle (*Emitte Spiritum Tuum*). The choir responded; two collects were read.

After this the novices received the kiss of peace, first from the superior, then from the brethren. Celebrant and ministers proceeded with the Mass. At the communion the newly clothed novices received the Eucharist. And from that moment on they became part of the monastic community.

Some decades later, in his work entitled *Chronicles of Mount St. Agnes,* Kempis made the following entry.

"In the year of our lord, 1406, on the Day of the Sacrament [feast of Corpus Christi], which was on the vigil of St. Barnabas [June 10] — it was a Thursday — three novices were clothed.

"As cleric, Thomas Hemerken of Kempen, diocese of Cologne, who happened to be the brother of John Kempen, first prior of the monastery; his father, John; his mother, Gertrude.

"Also as cleric, Octbert Wild of Zwolle; his father, Henry; his mother, Margaret.

"As lay brother, Arnold Droem / Drome of Utrecht; he brought with him many things of use to the monastery; he managed the dining room and was in charge of food services" (VII, 11, 371–72).

As for the year of novitiate that followed, it was more of the same but in greater detail and with greater intensity. — W.G.

4

Struggling

The kingdom of heaven is always under attack.

(Matthew 11:12)

Many begin the spiritual life; few make any progress; hardly any arrive at perfection. Why? We go with the flow when it comes to the flesh. We preen ourselves when it comes to pride. We crack up when things don't go our way. Alas, rare is the person who gets a hold on himself and expends all his energies seeking God alone and no other.

Yes, perfection is a rare bird, an elusive goal. It's just too hard to make war on one's self. The person who doesn't work hard at developing virtues will never be satisfied with the sweetness yielded by hard work. Every virtue has its own taste, a taste that satisfies, a pause that refreshes the one who harvests it.

The person who mucks around with vice is only creating a monster for himself. It snuffs honor, crinkles quiet, produces pain, increases sadness, ruins the taste of goodness forever.

The person who stays away from legitimate entertainment won't be so liable to fall for illegal entertainment.

The person who muzzles a junkyard dog won't have to worry about rabies.

The person who sews his lips together won't offend others with his remarks.

Always keep a good distance between yourself and lying, quarreling, detracting, insulting, and talking behind others' backs — the person who can do that will find silence somewhat easier and may some day come to enjoy it.

The person who hears no evil or sees no evil is unlikely to commit such evil.

Piety comes when the senses are well guarded, and so do the discipline of peace and the chapel of devotion.

When anger rages, wisdom flees for cover. The person who speaks wrathfully comes to resemble his dog. The person who responds in a suave, soothing way breaks the momentum of anger's fierce storm. Then angry thorns turn into crimson roses, and a pleasant blush returns to the cheeks of the afflicted.

Soothing also is the tongue of the prudent person; it heals the wounds of anger.

The person who resists vices when they rise will more easily repel borders when they attack.

The person who relies upon praying and meditating on celestial things joins the ranks of the Master Gardener; he plants roses and lilies in his field. Much pleasure lies in the immediate future of this person, mixing with the holy angels in the celestial garden.

A person may be said to be angelic who keeps his body and soul together in moments, even stretches, of duress.

A servant of the demons is the one who lives a life of vice and regales himself with rancid thought.

The fight to resist the allures of pleasure island is hard. But harder still will be the future punishment; no pleasure then, only eternal flame.

When love of God makes a grand entrance through the front, love of earth makes a hasty exit through the back.

The wise person is the one who could care less for a whole host of things.

All things amount to nothing; even the seal of a king and the bull of a pope are made of lead.

The end of all things? Warm ash in the shape of a worm.

In conclusion, whoever gambles with all earth's stuff should remember that death's the dealer that never loses.

Happy the pilgrim who has a warm bed and a hot meal awaiting him in heaven.

5

Acquiring

*Those of you who laugh
think you'll never cry.
That's where you're wrong!*

(Luke 6:25)

Virtue and vice — no bedfellows these! They're at each other's
throats. And it's no wonder. Vice is often acquired through
whimsical conversation in a casual, relaxed environment. Not
so with virtue. It can be acquired only through the grunt and
grind of hard work. It's not a group activity. It has to be
done alone.

No, virtue can't be acquired in a flash. It comes one step
at a time, and then only under stress and duress. There has
to be firm, unwavering dedication, always progressing toward
the far-off, invisible goal. Very often that means doing some
violence to oneself. That's to say, by fasting and watching and
praying and meditating and studying and writing and working
hard. That's also to say, by not wasting time with titillating
tales and not trumpeting your own horn.

Tears

Have you noticed that earthly joys enjoy only a half life? That's to say, that they don't last long? Right when you least expect it they expire, stain your clothes, offend your nose.

Weeping for joy or weeping for sadness — rarely will one or another of these two be absent from your life.

Roses

Good talk can be sweet to hear. Casual talk can upset a friend. Gruff talk can take the whiskers off a peach.

Be diligent in doing the good stuff. Be patient when it comes to enduring the bad stuff. Pray to God every hour on the hour. Do all these, and you'll live a very happy life.

A happy devout you'll be when you spelunk the junkyards of this world for your few worldly needs. Rare is the piece of junk that can't survive another, and indeed a better, use.

The devout who loves God accepts as coming from God the bitter with the sweet, knows whom to thank.

If you place your hope not in yourself but in God, then you're truly able to stand strong and tall.

∽∽∽∽∽∽

SOURCES OF WISDOM

Kempis was said to have copied the Scriptures four times, and hence he was totally familiar with such sources of revealed wisdom as Job, Proverbs, Ecclesiastes, and the letter of James.

To these must be added the Wisdom of Solomon and Ecclesiasticus or the Wisdom of Jesus Son of Sirach. These two weren't found in the surviving Hebrew Scriptures, but they were included in the Septuagint, a Greek translation of the Hebrew Scriptures. Honoring this distinction, the Reformation churches dropped Solomon and Sirach from their canon. Hence, the Hebrew list may be said to be protocanonical or first-canonical, and the Greek list deuterocanonical or second-canonical.

Of course, when Kempis lived and worked — he died in 1471 — the canon was one, and he freely quoted and excerpted all of these to great effect in his own books. Today the books from both scriptural lists are happily included and properly labeled in many English translations of the Bible, and in the New Revised Standard Version, which is referenced in this translation.

Add to these the personal wisdom of Gerard De Groote and Florent Radewijns, founders of the Brethren and Sistern of the Common Life, and Kempis had all the spiritual wisdom he needed to put together such anthologies, such treasuries, of spiritual wisdom as *Imitation of Christ, Soliloquy of a Soul, A Patch of Roses Somewhere in the Valley of Tears,* and *Valley of Lilies.*

—W.G.

6

Hearing

Blessed are those who hear the word of the Lord.

(Luke 11:28)

Trashy . . . that's what human solace is. That's because it gets in the way of solace divine.

When the sacred words of Scripture are read aloud, it's God's voice you hear. Drink it in; it'll give you a chill and at the same time fill you with warmth.

Truth isn't something you put in storage. Rather it's something you take out, dust off, and put on display. Nothing more needs to be done. Truth speaks for itself.

The person who lives the life of virtue is a model to us all. The same may be said of the person who reads the right stuff — he or she becomes another messenger of God.

The faithful messenger doesn't fuss over stuff that doesn't work; makes much ado about stuff that does work; above all, doesn't cook up stuff that isn't true.

Conversation with hidden meanings — one clean, the other not so clean — is harmful to children; flashiness always deceives.

The teller of tall tales is always a disturber of the peace. The person who hears scandal evades it not.

The judge who can hold his opinions to himself is worthy of all praise.

The person who deals unmercifully with others will find no mercy when his own case comes up.

The wrathful soul not only tortures itself but also does major damage to innocent bystanders; those stronger than himself he bad-mouths behind their backs; those who do good in public, he's in their face making fun of them.

Slick with words, often saying one thing but meaning another — that's the sort of person who deceives even the people who like and believe in him. No wonder his friends are an ever-decreasing circle.

There's no need to broadcast every bad thing that happens. It's a holy thing to sow the seeds of truth around. To conduct oneself modestly, without flash, without splash, is the only sensible thing to do.

If one wants to be thought just, he shouldn't step on another's toes. If pious, his friend should feel the richer for knowing him. If religious, he should help his neighbor's spiritual life with an appropriate word or deed whenever possible.

Prudent persons think before taking the plunge, don't follow the fashion in behavior or attire, shouldn't pass on rumors they don't know to be true.

Living the life of a good person brings peace to the heart, silence to the mouth. The fool's mouth, on the other hand, is always open, never closed, always ready for a cheap shot at someone else's expense.

The person who wants to please God should keep a close guard on his heart and mouth. Otherwise he'll not only lose the grace of devotion but also ruffle the feathers of those who cultivate the quiet life.

A torrent of words, no matter how beautiful, won't fill a sack, nor will a cataract of words, no matter how eloquent, confer meaning on the lives of the rich and famous.

All of which is another way of saying, the person who lives the spiritual life in this world will live the blessed life in the next.

7

Consoling

*The Lord is always close to those
who feel abandoned by him.*

(Psalm VUL 33:19; NRSV 34:19)

Anyone who's been on the pilgrimage trail even for a little while knows that he may be clobbered by desolation at any time. So when it happens, when your heart throbs with tribulation and heaves with grief, you need to know that you are with Jesus on the cross.

When consolation returns through the grace of the Holy Spirit, it's like rising from the dead with Jesus and walking out of the sepulcher; it's like eastering in the newness of life with Jesus celebrating in your heart.

When you hear someone aiming harsh and unforgiving words at you, it's like drinking from the chalice of the Lord — it's like medicine for your soul.

Don't say anything. Just down the drafts of salvation without a murmur. The foretaste may be awful but, surprisingly, the aftertaste isn't all that bad.

Remember and don't forget, whether in consolation or desolation, the Lord will be there for you both in life and death. The Lord won't forget you.

There's nothing grander than silence in the face of a withering barrage of insults. Just follow the example of the Christ in the presence of Pilate. Many false charges were hurled against him but, as Matthew pointed out, he held his tongue (26:63).

Don't worry about looking more attractive to the Lord. He already finds you attractive. After all, it was for you that he underwent flagellation and derision and finally death.

Human beings just don't know how good or virtuous they are until they've been stung by swarms of adversity.

Of course, Christ had many fine dinner companions — they could match him drink for drink, plate for plate — but only a few of them could undertake his abstinence even on a bet!

The true lover of the Crucified doesn't draw back because of the pain, nor lose his focus when confronted with perversity. Why? Because he's inspired to do what Christ did, conform to the scandal of the cross. That's what Paul wrote to the Philippians (1:21).

The more the love of God, the less the fear of God.

The more one desires to lose himself in Christ, the more he finds himself living happily with him and joyfully with the angels.

Happy the soul who loves Jesus from the bottom of his heart! He's the sort of one who counts present possessions as trash when compared to the eternal goods ahead.

For in the name of Jesus he does many things. He patiently puts up with evils. He prostrates himself humbly at the feet of Jesus. He prays that he might progress in virtue and stay the ragged course.

8

Rejoicing

Rejoice in the Lord always.

(Philippians 4:4)

Rejoice with the good stuff; put up with the bad stuff; suffer with the sick; pardon the delinquents; pray for everybody.

Don't dally with depression; it can lead to laziness and anger; flee from it as fast as you can.

Meditate on the life and passion of Christ, and you'll soon find enough consolation to dispel the darkest depression.

A good life deserves real praise. Gossip is a bore to yourself and others.

A good conscience generates joy; a bad conscience gives birth to depression.

Strive always to do well, and you'll soon find yourself in a good place.

Desperados won't lay a finger on you if you hold your course on the highway of the just.

Good human conversation brings with it joy of heart and fame of just praise.

Vain exultation is dead on arrival.

Especially harmful is the burbling praise of those who don't know any better.

Prayer rising from the salt of the earth to the highest heaven pleases God; it also implores grace and renounces the fraud of the devil.

Confession rising from the salt of the earth deserves forgiveness; frivolous excuse only aggravates the offense.

True contrition bleaches out the stain; sincere promise to sin no more lessens the punishment.

Explaining away a sin subtracts from the grace of devotion; a good and honest account of one's sins increases joy.

A cautious guard for the senses must be on duty at all times and in all places; this chaperon may even have to fence in the wandering soul.

Frequent prayer is a fine protection. A quiet mouth assures peace in the house.

Many begin fervently, but only perseverance wins the crown.

The burden Christ lays on people is sweet enough for those who love him but too heavy for those who loathe him; it's bitter for the proud and arrogant; light for the meek and mild; welcome for the humble and obedient.

Jesus makes everything sweet to the taste and light as a feather.

The carnal person seeks out the soft; the spiritual person detests and shuns the soft.

The just person is sad beyond belief because all the fires of vice can't be extinguished. So why does God permit this? In order to keep humankind forever humble and incessantly imploring divine help.

The really proud person rejoices in honors, and the really rich person exults in wealth. The truly humble person, on the other hand, draws joy from contempt of self and from few possessions.

What are the glory and the riches of the servants of God? Christ, the king of heaven.

Outside of God, all joy is junk; every abundance, a bust. Why? Nothing satisfies the famine of the soul, that's to say, except God alone who created the soul in the first place.

The great liberty of the soul? To lust for nothing that belongs to this world.

The life of the just person is to do good and endure evil; to praise God in all things; to enjoy the good things, yes, but not to take pride in them.

God truly likes best the person who thinks himself least. Whatever good that person thinks, speaks, does, he ascribes totally and faithfully to God.

What does that mean in practice?

When you're tempted by vainglory, you should withhold your consent. But more than that. You should humbly pray with the psalmist. "Not for us, O Lord, not for us, the glory that is yours" (VUL 113A:1; NRSV 115:1).

What's the greatest human accomplishment? To give up what's pleasing, attack what's terrifying, suffer slightly what's hurting greatly.

<hr />

FESTIVALS

Here is how historian Johan Huizinga viewed an important element of the society Kempis lived in.

In the Middle Ages the religious festival, because of its high qualities of style founded in the liturgy itself, for a long time dominated all the forms of collective cheerfulness. The popular festival, which had its own elements of beauty in song and dance, was linked up with those of the church.

It is toward the fifteenth century that an independent form of civil festival with a style of its own disengages itself from the ecclesiastical one. The "rhetoricians" of northern France and the Netherlands are the representatives of this evolution. Till then only princely courts had been able to equip secular festivals with form and style, thanks to the resources of their wealth and the social conception of courtesy. . . .

On the other hand, the ideas glorified by the secular feast were nothing more than those of chivalry and of courtly love. The ritual of chivalry, no doubt, was rich enough to give these festivities a venerable and solemn style. There were the accolade, the vows, the chapters of the orders, the rules of the tournaments, the formalities of homage, service, and precedence, all the dignified proceedings of kings-at-arms and heralds, all the brightness of blazonry and armor. But this did not suffice to satisfy all aspirations. The court fêtes were expected to visualize in its entirety the dream of the heroic life. And here style failed. For in the fifteenth century the apparatus of chivalrous fancy was no longer anything but vain contention and mere literature (Huizinga, *The Waning of the Middle Ages*, 251–52) — W.G.

9

Humbling

It's the humble that God gives the grace to.

(1 Peter 5:6)

Every act and every word of a humble religious brother or sister ought to be marked by a decoration on their religious habit. And there shouldn't be a trace of vanity about it.

One reliable sign of future probity in novices and postulants — they have modest habits, speak little, especially among the elders in their community.

The person who hasn't accustomed himself to silence, which just happens to be the first step of listening and learning, will rarely gain a reputation among those truly in the know.

Many are judged to be dunces because they have yet to cultivate the intellectual virtues.

To obey promptly, pray frequently, meditate devoutly, labor diligently, study broadly, avoid pontificating, love solitude: all these make a monk devout and his soul tranquil.

Remember that passage in Genesis? God showed his respect for Abel by giving him gifts. No such gifts were given to Cain. Why? He was envious of others and always took the opposite point of view (4:4–5).

When it comes to enduring some molestation to yourself, be Abel. Don't mess with Cain. You'll just lose your peace of mind and your reputation.

Rather than offend God or hurt your brother or sister or commit any other uncharitable act, dump your property.

If you want to make a deposit into the heavenly treasury, then toss your goods into the earthly trashery.

If you crave honors year after year, you should learn to devalue temporal glory.

If you want peace, not anger, then stay away from taverns and public houses. To be great in heaven, you must begin as a child on earth.

Don't bother justifying yourself out loud if all you can come up with is a bad conscience.

Audacity and bodacity, both of these are vituperative qualities, neither of which will get you on the straight and narrow.

Many brave persons have fallen because they overestimated their abilities.

Many sick have convalesced because they hoped in God and invoked his name.

The humble and well-mannered person? He makes himself or herself approachable to everyone.

The austere and rigid? They turn away everyone who approaches them.

The patient and taciturn? They conquer those who oppose them. Their only weapon? Charity.

Those who freely serve others and suffer with the suffering? They have more friends than they know what to do with.

Persons who don't know when or how to be silent? They give the appearance in public of being out of their mind.

The prudent? They know how to do good and have a command of the virtues. They know how to handle themselves when it comes to putting up a strong defense against vices.

Great is the Lord, he dominates depraved desires.

Brave is the soldier who tames the flesh, with continence as his chiefest weapon.

The person who lives chastely on earth deserves to be relocated with the angels in heaven. This same person is a friend of God's, and a chum of angels; virgins recognize him as one of them, and a beloved citizen of the saints.

The humble and chaste make short work of the demons; they're the living reproach to the proud and unchaste.

Great is the prelate who lives the life he preaches; he sets a good example for his subordinates. He is worthy of the praise of good people everywhere who try to follow the virtues of the good.

Beautiful is the person who is clean of sin.

Bad is the person who is flashy on the outside, fleshy on the inside.

He's happy and indeed rich who is full of the grace of God and desires no further honor.

Foolish the person is and indeed insane who harms himself by forgoing the medicine of the soul.

Wisdom it is to seek divine goods; they last longer than earthly goods.

If people show up on your doorstep and ask to be taught, show them the way of humility, and precede that by treating them humbly.

The truly humble person doesn't know how to blow things out of proportion. Praise means nothing to him; contempt, now that's something he can take pleasure in; insulted, he quickly brushes it off.

∽∾∽∾∽∾∽∾∽

PESSIMISM OR OPTIMISM

Historians of the Middle Ages — among them Cantor, Huizinga, Le Goff — have concentrated on the social well-being of the people and hence could see only pessimism, and why not? The religious communicators of the time reinforced this dark image since they too purveyed a type of pessimism, assigning little or no value to the things of this world. From Kempis's point of view, the people shouldn't want the things of this life even if they could have them.

In this very religious pessimism, however, lay religious optimism. Only those who hated the things of this world would enjoy the things of the next world. Only those who entered a rigorous spiritual regimen on earth would buy into this bifocular vision. But was it pessimism, or was it really a sort of optimism? Kempis thought it was the latter. He used the things of this world as a sort of rocket fuel to reach the next world. He looked forward to it, preached about it, and inculcated this bifocular vision in novices, postulants, whoever would listen.

Oddly, surprisingly, Kempis's heaven, if it didn't exactly look like earth, had the feel of earth, only the architecture was more splendid, the furniture more elegant, the personages more interesting, and so on. In other words, what had been abandoned here, at least in the way of material possessions, would be restored a thousandfold there.

Sadly, historians have rarely if ever been able to entertain this two-world vision. This is probably due to the fact that they haven't lived it themselves. Those medievals in the religious life believed it so, and so did Kempis. He saw that his job in all of his primers to the spiritual life — *Imitation, Consolations [Soliloquies], Roses, Lilies* — was to convince postulants and novices that it was indeed so.

By the way, these medieval meditations raised issues that are still of interest to modern contemplatives; only the details differ.

See everywhere in Kempis, but especially chapter 9, the present chapter, of *Roses.* —W.G.

10

Returning

You live with me, and I live with you,
and both of us will have a good time.

(John 15:5)

The thoughts and affections of humankind are all over the lot; various and unstable they are; but all the ones that are inane and impure don't come from God.

Human heart, why are you so relentless and yet so un-satisfiable! Remember what the prophet Jeremiah wrote? "To leave God behind is a bad, a bitter thing to do" (2:19).

Why do you fill up your mind with silly thoughts that have no staying power, no power to satisfy?

What you need to do is turn yourself around and live the good life. Reverse the direction your heart has been heading in. Make a checklist of all the bad things you've done. Do that, and you'll find yourself well on your own way to your heart's true home.

Here's a spiritual and mental exercise. Prepare your home, the place where your soul dwells, for a visit from God. Guard yourself from horrid images and calls for your attention. That's the only way to make room for the Holy Spirit.

The person who makes it a habit to go out in the world looking for excitement rarely improves his soul's lot.

All the worldly stuff parades proudly to a brilliant point in the distance; I think it's called the vanishing point.

Watching this parade doesn't satisfy the longing you feel. The parade sounds go in one ear and out the other, leaving the heart empty after as before. Now if the parade were going in the opposite direction and were full of praise for the Creator — these sights and sounds would begin to relieve your anxiety.

In this regard recall the holy David psalming at his lute. "I'm delighted at what you plan to do; I've already enjoyed the fruits of your work to date" (VUL 91:5; NRSV 92:4). These words are sung at lauds, the canonical hour at daybreak, in every church and monastery.

No one has sea legs in this wavering world; we all totter and tumble at the slightest wave; only in God's boat can we wobble but not fall down.

Stand in truth, and truth will free you from every lie and deception, and especially from the mythical story we all create about ourselves.

Rule of thumb. If everything you made up about your neighbor is bad, may he return the favor to you.

As John the evangelist put it, "Christ is the truth," and anyone who follows Christ has to be a lover of truth, and indeed of every other virtue (14:6).

Leave truth behind and invest heavily in earthly gain and the honors it brings, and you'll lose faith and the modesty virtue brings.

God is truth, and he doesn't allow liars to hide for long.

The alleged perpetrator can't cover up his life of lies for long. In the end the plainspoken will prevail. And the person with the overactive imagination won't know whether he's coming or going.

Don't cook up a desire for things that aren't right in their own right and hence aren't pleasing to God. I'm talking about virtues here. Good work as well as good works. Things done for the honor of God. That way you'll be welcomed by God and angels and the rest of humankind.

Fear not. The bad person can muscle up some transitory things for his amusement. But God won't be outdone; he'll return to the long-suffering person much, much more — and longer-lasting things.

If you want to have peace and good conscience, serve humility, patience, and obedience.

No one is a worse enemy to himself than himself. Proof of that is this. If you put your own defects under scrutiny, you'll soon come to see in them all the defects of humanity.

11

Falling

*Hope in the Lord, but at the same time
make something good happen.*

(Psalm VUL 36:3; NRSV 37:3)

No one gets too excited about his furniture; no one gets too chummy with his friends and relatives. That's because everything is so uncertain and so unsafe.

However, the person who puts his confidence in the Lord will raise a shout every time he finds himself in trouble. No matter what the source of the noise, the Lord will come.

A great sense of peace comes over a person who does his spiritual life well, speaks only good about his neighbor, hurts no one's feelings, puts up a defense against all incoming iniquitous and ubiquitous thoughts.

Sometimes just closing the door will restore peace to a room or a house.

The person who sins most often is the one who hasn't had a pious thought in his head or his heart for days; that's to say, he's let his guard down enough for Satan to slip through the lines. People like that stop praying. Odd thing, that. Without the grunt and grind of spiritual exercise, good virtue can't be built.

A knight of the road is abashed by the narrowness of a monastery in the same way a bird is afraid of a cage.

When you find yourself tempted heavily or derided openly or confused inwardly or despised generally, don't despair. Just remember that such small iniquity as you may have stored up in the past deserves some whipping.

Keep on keeping on; be patient and speak confidently. As the psalmist has sung, "Level me from time to time, Lord; how else will I learn to behave?" (VUL 118:71; NRSV 119:71).

Reeling from the gravity of his infractions, a fellow finds himself in a teachable moment. He learns that he needs God and needs him fast!

Fatuous and unfaithful is the servant who lords it over the goods of the Lord and looks down on others who have no goods whatsoever.

Despising those who serve with him and thinking himself better than they, a fellow sends the wrong aroma heavenward. Should this same spiritual error arise in us, it's a sure sign that we aren't humble and haven't been paying attention to our own defects. We should never let our guard down. In fact, we should never stop up our tears of contrition.

Everyone carries a load that is his alone. So why does he carry more than he can bear? And why does he dump on the deeds of others?

It happens, someone falling or erring or neglecting something. His confusion compounds the humiliation he feels for this public act. At a moment like that we feel sorry for a bloke, but that only makes it worse for the person who was caught *in flagrante delicto*. When such a thing happens, a person may resort to the most extraordinary excuses.

54

"I'm only a human being!"

"I'm not an angel!"

"It could have happened to anybody!"

To the public sinner we're brothers and sisters. We've all sinned, and at the same time all pretend we haven't.

Who has never wandered or squandered? Only God. So why do we laugh at the slip of another? Yes, we're still standing, as Paul wrote in his first to the Corinthians, but how do we know our turn to fall isn't coming right up? (10:12).

One last thing. Confusion often runs riot — but from the point of view of spirituality is that necessarily a bad thing? It certainly brings us down a peg.

ROSES IN SCRIPTURE

Roses as Kempis wrote about them have any number of meanings, not the least of which is roses as they appear in the Scripture. Two Bible dictionaries shed some light.

Revell Bible Dictionary

The "rose" of Scripture is not the flower called by that name today. In Isaiah 35:1, the flower is probably the crocus (as in the NIV), which bursts into bloom after an infrequent desert rain. Most take the "rose of Sharon" in Solomon's great love poem as the narcissus or perhaps a tulip. Both of these plants grow in the highlands around Sharon and are valued garden plants (876).

Harper Bible Dictionary

The rose by the brook (Ecclesiasticus 39:13) and the rose plants of Jericho (Ecclesiasticus 24:14) most likely refer to the oleander bush (Nerium oleander), a plant with shiny, leathery evergreen leaves and large deep pink or white flowers. Growing along wadis (dry riverbeds) and other watercourses, the oleander is an outstanding feature of the otherwise arid countryside all over the Holy Land. It is also widely cultivated today in city parks and gardens (948). —W.G.

12

Praying

Pray and pray and pray some more.

(1 Thessalonians 5:17)

Continuous prayer might have been good for Paul's Thessalonians, but that was fourteen hundred years ago, and this is now. Would it be good for us? Well, yes. We have the same tribulations and temptations as the Thessalonians, the same insidious traps and inroads made by the bad angels.

Rarely do we hear news about what's good in the world. It's all bad news really. Wars and rumors of wars — that sort of thing. Fears inside the house, battles outside. No day passes without the grime of war; no hour, without the horror of death.

So what else can we conclude about God's just judgment but that wars and fires come because of the sins of humankind? Small consolation, that. But the elect should consider such flagellation as the price one pays in seeking celestial goals.

All this having been said, continuous prayer, prayer without stop, would seem to be of the greatest importance. It's the only thing we can do in a world full of perils. I mean, prayer is the only shield strong enough to withstand the enemy pikes.

The person who chooses not to pray chooses also to stay at home and not to engage in battle. And those who choose not to enjoin the battle are quickly overrun and lose their earthly crowns.

Who can spend all their time praying and fighting? Well, the person who invokes God for help and puts his trust in him can do anything. The psalmist confirmed this. "The Lord is never far away from those who call his name and really mean it" (VUL 144:18; NRSV 145:18).

If you can't cry for help out loud, you can always shout in prayer. Whichever, pray with desire and right intention.

Continue making sacrifices on the altar of your heart. That'll always reveal the goodwill of one trying to do the right spiritual thing, that's to say, always serving God. Of course, the person who always tries to do the spiritual thing well is already in a continuous state of prayer.

The person who troubles himself about his past sins is also the sort of person who'll groan for future goods; in other words, shifting from one to the other and back again doesn't break the continuity of prayer in his life.

Pray with holy David in this psalm of his. "I've let you know my every desire, Lord; and I've made no secret of my every distress" (VUL 37:10; NRSV 38:9).

In this regard, you'll find immensely useful the sermon of God as it's contained in the Sacred Scriptures; it's a must when trying to recollect one's soul, grown hairier with each successive passion.

Reading reveals the right way for a spiritual or religious person to live; it offers examples of people who've done it before, and prayer begs the grace to imitate them.

Spiritual reading is good, but prayer is better; best of all is when God is the cause and goal of it all.

Blessed is the person who orders all his words and deeds toward the praise of God; that's the way a beatitude should end, that God may be all in all, blessed from above and praised forever.

But just how can a person who prefers tall tales and mischievous myths to reading the Bible become a religious and a devout? Now that you're here as postulant and novice, how can you persevere?

A light-headed and sometimes light-fingered young man tends to sell his soul short.

When tribulation and temptation enter your spiritual life, make a mad dash back to your prayer place, pull up the drawbridge and let down the portcullis, and start screaming to high heaven for help.

The sooner, the better; the slower, the badder. The oftener it happens, the handier you become in meeting it. The ferventer you are, the welcomer you'll be to God.

The pious and merciful God wants to be asked; he sets out any number of reasons to pray for his help; he promises us a prompt response. Remember, Jesus said it. "Ask, and I'll give it to you." At least two evangelists were within earshot that day (Matthew 7:7; Luke 11:9).

He encouraged us to do so, offered examples of how to do it, threatened punishment if you didn't, offered complimentary gifts if you did, gave those who didn't a rough time, cheered up those who did. And then, if I may echo the genesist, "That was evening, and that was morning, of day one in your spiritual life" (1:5).

Often God conducts an experiment, a trial run, of extreme delicacy upon those who pray devoutly. This isn't well understood by the masses. To those who pray, however, it's a well-known phenomenon. As for those who read finicky novels and flounce about at tacky shrines, they haven't a clue.

WAR

In the present chapter, "Praying," Kempis mentions yet another unpleasant aspect of medieval life, "wars and rumors of war." Here is how the historian Huizinga saw it.

At the end of the fourteenth century and at the beginning of the fifteenth, the political stage of the kingdoms of Europe was so crowded with fierce and tragic conflicts....

In England, King Richard dethroned and next secretly murdered, while nearly at the same time the highest monarch in Christendom, his brother-in-law Wenzel, king of the Romans, is deposed by the electors.

In France a mad king and soon afterward fierce party strife, openly breaking out with the appalling murder of Louis of Orléans in 1407, and indefinitely prolonged by the retaliation of 1419 when Jean sans Peur is murdered at Montereau.

With their endless train of hostility and vengeance, these two murders have given to the history of France, during a whole century, a somber tone of hatred. It finds no explanation for [these] historic events save in personal quarrels and motives of passion.

In addition to all these evils came the increasing obsession of the Turkish peril, and the still vivid recollection of the catastrophe of Nicopolis in 1396, where a reckless attempt to save Christendom had ended in the wholesale slaughter of French chivalry.

Lastly, the great schism of the West had lasted already for a quarter of a century, unsettling all notions about the stability of the church, dividing every land and community. Two, soon three, claimants for the papacy! (17–18).

In the feudal age the private wars between two families have no other discernible reason than rivalry of rank and covetousness of possessions. Racial pride, thirst of vengeance, fidelity, [these] are their primary and direct motives. There are no grounds to ascribe another economic basis to them than mere greed of one's neighbor's riches (22). —W.G.

13

Reading

You mean to say,
you haven't read what God wrote
specifically for you?
(Matthew 22:31)

Sometimes people are desperate for a bit of good news. Odd thing, that, for there's always a fair amount of such news available at all hours. I refer to the Scriptures, and in them Christ speaking about the kingdom of God, the judgment to come, the heavenly Jerusalem, the happiness of the heavenly citizenry, the orders and choirs of angels rejoicing nonstop forever.

Then there are the prophets announcing the mysteries of Christ, intoning the punishments for sinners.

The apostles and evangelists disclosing in detail the works and miracles of Christ.

The doctors of the church sermonizing from pulpits galore, making cloudy passages clear, offering examples of the Christian life, refuting heresies, and rectifying errors.

Please note. Readers should pick and choose. But they shouldn't reject something on the ground that it's too simple to be believed, not complex enough to be considered. To dump on the wisdom of our forebears, or to reconsider the divines and the saints — that's just bonkers.

Some hard-won wisdom.

First, work hard at fulfilling small, seemingly inconsequential obligations and duties. Then God will give you greater tasks with intellectual dimensions.

"To know something and not to do it — that's a sin," according to the Letter of James (4:17).

A person may know and read much, but if he doesn't put his knowledge into action, he leaves the groaning board without a morsel.

On the one hand, the person who prays a little and labors not a whole lot will remain a pauper and a pooper. On the other hand, the person who rebukes vices in his public life and resists them in his private life has broadcast good seeds among the thorns.

The person who prays a lot of words will harvest little fruit; alas, he hasn't used prayer to fortify his heart against the onslaughts of depraved thoughts.

Happy the soul who guards itself against streams of impurity! This person doesn't brook any delay in dusting up his inmost heart, desperately searching for the slightest fault in the eyes of God.

Confession of sins before God himself will purge all vices from the humble and contrite heart.

The devout delight in prayers; the studious, in books; the virtuous, in good thoughts and deeds; the proud, in honors and decorations; the humble, in modest surroundings; the rich, in stately homes; the mendicant, in alms; the gluttonous, in food and drink; the leisurely, in novels; the sober, in abstinence; the wise, in wisdom; the good monk, in the discipline of everyday life. Ranking above all these in joy and delight are the love of God and a good conscience.

To rid the soul of your wicked-most thoughts, you can do three things. Flee for your life, zip your lips, settle down to a regular spiritual life. And while you're at this trivium, do try the quadrivium. Pray, fast, study, work.

Character traits.

The holy person thinks holy thoughts, speaks true things, deals fairly with others, ignores the present, concentrates on the eternal.

The humble listen to counsels; the prudent avoid dangers; the patient keep tribs and troubs close to their vest; the diligent don't neglect their daily rounds.

Four personalities.

The person who doesn't pick up small things will trip over large ones.

The person who's devotion is tepid in the morning is unlikely to grow more fervent by evening.

The person who tries to yank himself out of torpor and plunge himself into labor will acquire great joy and honor for himself — if not from others, then certainly from God. He's the reward of all hard work and the perpetual crown of the saints.

Lastly, the leisured class won't be satisfied with novels or other made-up accounts. The virtuous will abstain even from the things they're allowed.

They walk straight and tall who are humble right down to their boots; they count the gleaming honors of the world as tiddlywinks.

Wise is as wise does when it comes to pleasing God alone. And so if one wants to be considered a wisdom figure, he should flee the outside world, seek the interior life, develop an appetite for celestial stuff and a distaste for earthly dishes, lower his self-esteem, but not to an unhealthy level. That's the sort of person who always puts the love of God at the top of his list.

∿∿∿∿∿∿∿

ANOTHER WAY OF COPYING THE BIBLE

Up to the middle of the fifteenth century the only way to copy a Bible was by hand. That was the way Kempis did it, and he did it four times. Yet within a hundred miles of Mount St. Agnes, in Mainz, another copyist was hard at work producing the same Bible, the Latin Vulgate, but not by pen and ink.

Johann Gensfleisch (John Gooseflesh) was his name, but he preferred to be called Johann Gutenberg (Goodmountain). He was born a German and spent much of his life in the brackish territories between Germany and France. He was a tinker and technician with an inventor's imagination, mastering a number of arts dealing with stone, wood, and metal.

Gutenberg began with wood. A block of wood for each page of text. Each letter was carved out of the wood. He inked the letters and put paper to ink, and the result was a printed page. Granted, the hand-copyist could finish a page more quickly than a whittler could cut the letters for that page, but the whittler could produce ten block Bibles faster than the scrivening monks ten Bible manuscripts.

To streamline this process he decided to cut each letter on a letter-sized block and form words with the movable letters. Wood was a good medium, but if Gutenberg wanted to produce books in quantity, he needed a more durable substance. Metal it became.

Finally, he applied the movable wooden-letter technology to metal, set the letters on a line, putting anywhere from thirty-two to forty-two lines on one page frame, and the pages were ready to be printed on lumbering wooden presses.

In Mainz, between 1450 and 1455, the "Gutenberg" Bible was published, two hundred copies on rag cotton linen paper, thirty copies on vellum. It was the beginning of a revolution that would spread the word of both God and man.

In 1534 the first Lutheran Bible was published, fulfilling at least part of Luther's master plan; it is generally conceded that it is a masterpiece of German prose literature.

In England around the turn of the seventeenth century, two major English translations appeared.

In 1582 Catholic scholars working from Jerome's Latin Vulgate published the New Testament in Rheims. In 1610 they published the Old Testament in Douai, then in the Spanish Netherlands, now a part of France.

In 1611 Protestant scholars working from the original languages (Hebrew and Greek) produced the 1611 King James Bible; it was also known as the King James Version.

The English of the King James Version has long been thought stylistically superior to that of the Douai-Rheims Version. But truth to tell, the translators of both came from the same talent pool, the English universities, and hence they were marvelously educated and splendidly fluent with and in their native tongue. Hence, I think it safe to say that these fairly anonymous gents, Protestants as well as Catholics, did as much for the burgeoning English language as their contemporary, the great Shakespeare himself. — W.G.

14

Loving

Let charity be the key word in all you do.
(1 Corinthians 16:14)

Charity is noble. Charity lords it over all virtues, all branches of knowledge, all supernatural gifts.

Why?

Charity embraces God.

Charity associates angelic beings with human beings.

Charity takes children of humankind and makes them children of God and friends of saints.

Charity made it possible for Christ to be born of a virgin and crucified for human salvation.

Charity purifies the soul from sin, and draws one up to love God with whole heart, soul, and mind; with a sweetness that must be admired, it fills and raises.

Charity makes honest people out of dishonest, free people out of slaves, friends out of enemies, citizens out of immigrants, families out of strangers, homebodies out of vagabonds.

Charity makes humble people out of proud, meek out of perverse, fervid out of tepid, joyful out of sad, generous out of miserly, heaven bound out of earthbound.

"Charity — that's what makes all this spiritual activity work," according to Paul in his letter to the Romans; "charity poured into the hearts of believers everywhere; a gift to them from heaven through the Holy Spirit" (5:5).

Charity has wings that are as broad as they are long, wings that fly over cherubim and seraphim, above all the choirs of angels.

Charity joins the highest with the lowest, passes through intermediate realms but always returns to the highest perch.

Charity makes one out of many; the crowd rejoices, and it leaves a nice afterglow in each and every one.

Charity has no existence to boast of by itself; it's not a single, solitary thing, but it exceeds all other things in divine love.

Charity makes the rounds of heaven and earth, ocean and desert; everything it sees and hears in creatures, it reflects back to the praise and glory of the Creator.

Charity makes the devout soul praise God, thus producing benediction, exultation, jubilation.

Through charity the souls burns within and, like wax under flame, turns into liquid.

Charity doesn't know where its boundaries are, but it flies above all luminaries.

Charity helps in the valiant battle against daily temptation. Desolation suddenly and rudely comes, after moments of great consolation; a sudden temptation, a skin laceration, a humongous health problem, a loss of friends, and then there's enemy invasion, mental disease; and I mustn't forget the derision of children or the infirmity of the elderly, or a stiff reprimand from the local prelate.

Charity has something to do with all these, if only in humbling the pride in our heart, showing how we share the suffering of the tribulations and temptations. We really don't have confidence in ourselves, nor does wisdom seem to cover every situation, nor do the old rules always seem to apply. But in all things let us humble ourselves and "subject ourselves to God" as well as to the local authorities (2:13).

Through charity God has done many things. He came into the world. He led humankind back to heaven. He descended to the lowest level of man the sinner. He ascended the ignominy of the cross on the way back to the right hand of the Father. He gave humankind the greatest honor possible, that's to say, salvation.

Charity never takes a day off. It effects great and sublime things; has no trouble with lowly chores and duties.

Charity is honest in that perfection is its destination. It doesn't blush when it has to brush with the lowest of the low, especially under obedience. It doesn't shrink from touching wounds, washing feet, making beds, laundering clothes, scrubbing stains. To tough jobs charity brings patience, never loses joy amid the opprobrium.

As fire consumes wood, so charity extinguishes vice. It cleanses the heart through contrition, rinses the heart through confession, towels off with prayer, illumines through sacred reading, ascends through devout meditation, comes together in a private place, joins the soul to God through fervent love.

Charity prompts the mouth to praise God, the hand to do work, the feet to walk, the eyes to contemplate, the memory to remember; the exterior members to serve, the interior gifts to love God over all goods in heaven and on earth.

This charity I've been talking about has repercussions. In a humble soul it deletes past sins, fortifies against future sins, instructs about current sins. It liberates the doubters, discourages the curious, cuts off the superfluous, excludes vanity, takes issue with falsity, debunks bunkum, takes the pressure off of hard stuff, illuminates obscurity, opens the secrets of heaven to the one praying, orders all things inside as well as outside.

Charity is goodwill in a holy soul that doesn't get in the way of working properly. Of course, debility and necessity sometimes prevent the good stuff we planned to do from ever being done. During moments like this everything tastes bitter; everything feels itchy.

Such God requires. Such God loves. A soul who abandons itself and all things for his love. It fights bravely, and holds his heart in purity.

Quickly and freely the pure soul heads toward God; it flies above all the creations in the sky. But while on earth it has no wants or needs.

The charity of Christ breaks all earthly chains, undoes all sailors' knots. It makes heavy burdens light, but fulfills whatever obligations God places on us.

Whence this quotation from Christ as Matthew recorded it. "Not my will but yours." It's applicable anywhere and everywhere (26:42).

CARITAS AND AGAPE

Kempis wasn't the first to write about charity (*caritas* in Latin, *agape* in Greek), and he certainly won't be the last. But what he has written about this theological virtue compares most favorably, I think, with what the apostle Paul wrote in the first century of the Christian era and what C. S. Lewis wrote in the twentieth.

First, Paul, as paraphrased from the Latin Vulgate, the Bible Kempis used.

If I speak like an angel or rant like a rhetorician but don't have a charitable thing to say, I might as well be a bell hammered or a cymbal struck.

If I speak like a prophet or make like a magus, even if I pontificate like a professor or move mountains like game pieces, but don't have a whiff of charity about me, I'm a flop.

If I convert my wealth into food for the poor or offer myself up as a living sacrifice but keep charity at arm's length, I'm a complete bust.

Charity puts up with a lot but smiles in return. It doesn't overestimate itself, make wrong turns, magnify itself out of all proportion, look in the mirror much, needle its neighbor, entertain evil thoughts, rejoice when evil wins a tiff. Quite the contrary, charity enjoys its time with truth, but suffers and believes and hopes and endures everything else (1 Corinthians 13:1–7).

Lewis, next, taken from *The Four Loves.*

God is love. Again, . . . Herein is love, not that we loved God but that he loved us (1 John 4:10). We must not begin with mysticism, with the creature's love for God, or with the wonderful foretastes of the fruition of God vouchsafed to some in their earthly life.

We begin at the real beginning, with love as the divine energy. This primal love is gift-love. In God there is no hunger that needs to be filled, only plenteousness that desires to give.

The doctrine that God was under no necessity to create is not a piece of dry scholastic speculation. It is essential. Without it we can hardly avoid the conception of what I can only call a "managerial" God; a Being whose function or nature is to "run" the universe, who stands to it as a headmaster to a school or a hotelier to a hotel. . . .

If I may dare the biological image, God is a "host" who deliberately creates his own parasites; causes us to be what we may exploit and "take advantage of" him. Herein is love. This is the diagram of love himself, the inventor of all loves ("Charity," The Four Loves [New York: Harcourt, Brace, 1960], 175–76). — W.G.

15

Watching

Put up a good fight,
and the devil will take to his heels.
(James 4:7)

As a good devout, you too should be preoccupied with God. How? By praying and meditating and studying and writing. When you do that, present in the room with you are holy angels rejoicing. Also present with you, tempting and distracting, are the devils.

When you devouts pray, the devils flee as if to avoid the searing touch of the Holy Spirit. But when you gossip, the devils quickly return and with a bundle of fresh, even more inane, rumors.

When the prefect suddenly returns to this writing room, he'll waggle his finger at the chatsters and neglecters of good works, and silence will steal back into the room.

What can we draw from this?

Why don't we, then, just let the silence continue? If we must have some solace every now and then, just think of God. That'll free you from the tedium that always seems to accompany good work and good works. That'll encourage you to persevere.

Tears

Be faithful in the small details now, and then you'll discover a bundle under your name in the heavenly treasury.

Whether you're alone or with others, you can never let your guard down. You have to fight, watch, pray that temptations of the flesh and the spirit don't swarm over the rampart.

Put up a good fight if it comes to that. Pray fervently. Labor diligently. Don't lapse into talk. Don't get testy. Endure patiently.

Roses

If you're not chatty in private, then you won't be catty in public. Confounded by your unwillingness to keep up a constant chatter, the devil will leave in a huff. You see, there's one sort of person he hates — a devout who keeps to himself while he works in the writing room and who's recollected in the praying room.

No matter how discombobulated you become, always put your hope in the Lord.

Every time you meet a difficult situation head on, my dear devout, rally around the virtue of patience. That way, victory and peace may be yours now. That's the way in the future you'll be awarded the glorious crown of the elect.

16

Hauling

His burden is your burden too.

(Galatians 6:2)

We're all one in Christ, and from that proposition flows another. Charity begins at home. We ought to hold familial and fraternal charity in an unending and unbreakable chain of peace.

Remember, we're all members of Christ, reborn in baptism through the grace of the Holy Spirit, redeemed by the passion of Christ, bathed in the blood of Christ, fed with the body of Christ, educated in the words of Christ, confirmed in the miracles of Christ, motivated by the examples of Christ.

So now I can put it to you, my brothers in Christ, would you do anything to hurt each other? Who would deliberately lay low another with a word or a deed? The person who did that would offend Christ.

A solemn note. Remember, Christ will have his judgment, and Christ will have his punishment unless the offending devout makes haste to reform his life.

We have God the Father in heaven; we have all sorts of brothers and sisters in Christ here on earth, gathered together here from whatever city or state, of whatever parentage, from the noble to the not-so-noble.

One God has created us all, fed us and set our course, called us to one and the same beatitude; and he renews that call daily. How? By exhortations from without, through contrition from within. This same God has promised to see us through to the eternal reward ceremonies, with standing ovations from all the heavenly citizens.

If therefore we've been unanimously called by God, redeemed for one price, drunk from one Spirit, then let's love and help each other.

If we want to please Christ, then for him we'll heft each other's burdens, whatever they may turn out to be. Out of charity we'll pray for each other. That's because God is in us, and we in him.

No matter how imperfect or inept we find a fellow, we ought to err on the side of good interpretation rather than bad — that's what we'd hope for ourselves.

Fine fellows all, help with your brothers' burdens, and they'll return the favor. Give them the benefit of the doubt, and no doubt they'll return it.

Have compassion for the sinner, and you'll have his, next time you commit a howler.

Console the mournful, and you'll be consoled by the cheerful.

Pick up a fallen friend, and guess who'll pick you up next time you fall? God himself.

So it seems quite clear. What you do for another will be done for you by another; that's how the just God runs his court.

Don't be surprised, or think it beneath contempt, when a fragile human being falls in this world. An angel fell in heaven. Adam fell in the paradise; an apple did him in; not a prizewinner, it had a worm in it.

Often it's the small thing that trips a person up, or provokes another person to trip you up. This, God justly permits to happen; all he wants you to know is the truth about yourself, that you're not as sure-footed as you thought you were. And that's with a small provocation. Against a large provocation you haven't got a chance.

Don't blow your top when a brother is in the throes of temptation. Pray for the troubled person because he can't pray for himself, just as you'd pray for yourself.

Your good is my good through mutual agreement; and likewise your evil is my evil through mutual compassion.

Truth is, we're all fragile; we're all crockery; we all break when we hit the floor. That's why we pray out of charity for each other.

So much about helping, but what about not helping?

Don't be too quick to point out a defect in another. If you had that very same defect, then it would be like the blind leading the blind, the deaf shouting insults to the deaf, the stupid deriding the stupid for being stupid.

Above all, don't bad-mouth a person who's done nothing bad to you. Instead, take a close look at his defect, and you may very well find that you're seeing a mirror image; that's to say, that you are the proud possessor of that very same defect! Don't correct him before you correct yourself.

If you rightly judge and intend to correct your neighbor, begin with yourself. And then proceed to your neighbor, but do it without commotion. There's no need to bust up his furniture; rearrange it, perhaps, but discreetly, tastefully.

Simply put, where there's sincere and fraternal love, then you'll suffer with me as I with you, and the same with prayer.

The person who causes another to fall is cruel, an enemy, not the sort of one you'd want to call for help in an emergency; that person's just a shaggy sermonizer.

Actually, the person who prays for another as he prays for himself accomplishes quite a bit. The more fraternal charity one has, the more he'll pray for his friend, and the quicker his friend will respond. And, as God would have it, his friend will never be the wiser.

A caution. The more one suffers with a bad brother who won't hear a word said against himself, the less it's worth the while of the brother trying to help.

A final word about an afflicted friend. For all your efforts you're going to come off as either a redolent rose or a bloody thorn.

17

Staying

Don't go — please stay!
(John 15:9)

Christ's voice is sweet to the ear. It's the sort of sound one wants to follow and obey.

The love of Christ produces happiness of mind, paradise of soul. It locks out the world, overcomes the devil, shuts the gate of hell, opens the gate of heaven.

Please note. Love of Christ and love of world are contraries; they have nothing in common, nor can they be in the same room at the same time.

Love of Christ is the four-horser of Elias rising to heaven; love of the world is a four-wheeler of the devil's, hauling people to hell.

Love of self is a self-inflicted wound; oblivion of the world is a heavenly invention.

The sweet-talking and slipsiding of an imagined friend do more damage than the straightforward, in-your-face corruption of an honest person.

The fast-talking purveyor of dubious goods uses statements that aren't true; the logical mind of a just person always proceeds from cause to effect.

The person who springs scandal upon another person can't evade the charge of scandal himself.

God, chief executive and financial officer of all creation, doesn't allow so much as a bleating lamb to wander off for long; he either cudgels it back with a shepherd's crook or merely beckons it back with a kindly eye.

Where peace and concord are, there God is with his treasury of graces.

Where litigation and dissension are, there the devil is with his bag of tricks.

"Where there's humility," reads the Book of Proverbs, "there's wisdom. And where there's pride, there's malice" (11:2). Conquer the pride, and you'll find great peace.

Where sharp words are exchanged, poor charity is left bleeding in the street.

Where solitude and silence reign, there the quiet sounds of happy monks.

Where labor and discipline are alive and well, there the religious making spiritual progress live.

Where laughter and horsing around abound, there devotion has fled the premises.

The otiose and the verbose are rarely roused; the pure are rarely close to sin.

Where obedience is prompt, conscience is content.

Where tall tales rule the roost, there negligence to the rule has taken hold.

Where there's charity toward self, there's sure to be a lack of charity toward others.

Where doctrine flourishes, salvation increases.

Where concord rules, sound is sweet.

Where mediocrity pours the grape, there concord's days are numbered.

Where discretion in correcting faults is maintained, there no one should complain, nor should the local prelate blow his top.

What's the meaning of all this?

Yes, everything ought to be kicked up a notch; there's always room at the top for an outstanding virtue.

Where patience lies in wait, eventual victory over the enemy is assured.

When clamor lumbers in the front door, peace tiptoes out the back door.

Shut your mouth before you blow your cool.

Where faith and truth hang out, there you'll find peace and security.

Where double-speak and double-deal abound, there you will find stunted mental development and prudence wearing blinkers.

Where charity, there the Holy Spirit.

Where quick suspicion, there frequent confrontation.

Where people know truth, there joyful hearts abound.

Where people make up stories as excuses, they often deceive their own friends.

Where there's humble confession, there's genuine forgiveness.

Wherever earthly wisdom comes up short, divine protection fills in the gap.

Whoever brings bad things to other things will come to a bad end himself.

Peace to those who do much in the spiritual life well and fortify themselves with patience.

Woe to the imposter who does evil and to the pretender who feigns good! Hasn't it been true that iniquity hurts no one more than the perpetrator? Where duplicity is found under the carpet, there also are such verminous friends as inconstancy and wickedness; an echo from the Letter of James (1:8).

The simple and the just live without guile because God is with them, clearing the traffic on the Via Justitativa.

He who makes bad use of the word of God runs a great risk; once spotted as the fraud he is, who will believe him again? The person who changes his tune for the better won't infringe on the truth.

How good it is to hear good news! How much better it is to do good works! Best of all is conversation that results in change of life — abstinence from sin, progress in virtue, that sort of thing.

The fruit of devout prayer? To unite a heart with God in the fervor of the Holy Spirit.

A prayer is devout when it excludes all extraneous pictures and conversations.

The person who uses an image of Christ in his prayer quickly drives out the diabolical flimflam that usually clutters the prayer life.

A suitable prayer image for those staggering under their daily loads? Christ carrying the cross.

The person who carries the sacred wounds of Jesus around today cauterizes and heals the wounds of the mind.

The person who puts a low value on earthly things has no desire for medals and decorations, no heart for eulogies or elegies, no mind for anything but God.

Over and above the chatter in God's ear trumpet, coming through loud and clear, is the true contrition of the heart from the mouth of a humble sinner.

Whatever good you do, do it for God's eyes only.

The person who defers to God his virtues and good works, attributes nothing to his own merits or efforts. On the contrary he dumps the stuff out and denudes himself of them. Pride, envy, vainglory he merely fumigates.

Why? The person who deprives himself of eternal glory and honor is the sort who finds joy only in himself and not in God, who just happens to be the greatest good.

How to respond to a gift like this?

This is how the blessed virgin Mary responded to a supreme gift from above. In a canticle, a jubilant song, at least as recorded by Luke in his gospel. "My spirit has rejoiced in God my savior" (1:47).

This is how Paul put it in his to the Galatians. "The person who truly thinks he amounts to something when in reality he doesn't has, alas, seduced himself" (6:3).

Getting swept up into third heaven doesn't count for much. Attributing all to God — now that's something to get excited about.

"Wherever I am," wrote Paul in his first to the Corinthians, "I've arrived by the grace of God" (15:10).

LEGEND OF ST. AGNES

Kempis's Augustinian monastery was dedicated to St. Agnes, one of the most popular Christian saints then and now. She died in A.D. 304 or 305. She, along with Felicitas, Perpetua, Agatha, Lucy, Cecilia, and Anastasia, were all virgin martyrs from the early days of Christianity. They were commemorated daily in the Roman Mass until the Second Vatican Council (1962–65); they still remain as an option within an option. That's to say, as a option in the first of the four eucharistic prayers, any one of which a priest may choose on any day of the church year.

This is approximately what Kempis and his fellow monks knew of Agnes in the middle of the fifteenth century.

Born of a patrician Roman family who had converted to Christianity, Agnes was barely more than a child when she was sought after by the noble pagans. She replied that her heart was already spoken for, and that her virginity was consecrated to a heavenly husband, Jesus Christ. Angered, the young men turned her over as a Christian to the pagan government of Emperor Diocletian. At first she was in protective custody where she was encouraged to change her mind. Instruments of torture were paraded before her, but she laughed at them. Then she was dragged before some Roman gods where, if she wanted to survive, she'd have to offer incense; she raised her hand, but it was to make the sign of the cross. Next, she was committed to a house of prostitution, and her availability to the youth of Rome was announced publicly. Only one out of the mob of pubescent youngsters who came out to deflower her dared approach. When he touched her, he was struck blind. By her immediate intercession, his sight was restored. The government then condemned her to beheading.

Contemporary reports had it that she went to the beheading as though she were heading for her wedding. One easy stroke from the headsman, and she was gone.

So much for what Kempis knew. No doubt he suspected that the details of the story had been rounded off. But then again hagiography, the art and science of writing biographies of saints, would take centuries to mature enough to determine fact from fiction in the lives of saints like Agnes. Of course, no medieval person would go to hell if he or she swallowed the Agnes legend whole.

Looking back on this account from the twenty-first century, we can place little reliance on the details of this story. For example, according to Ambrose she was beheaded; according to Pope Damasus, she was burned to death; according to a contemporary hymn she was strangled. According to Thurston and Attwater's revision of *Butler's Lives of the Saints* and to Farmer's *Oxford Dictionary of Saints,* Agnes was stabbed in the throat or breast, not a pretty picture, but it was regarded as the most merciful form of coup de grâce.

No doubt Agnes existed. No doubt she died in A.D. 304 or 305. No doubt a basilica was erected in her honor in 354. No doubt her name appears in a 354 document entitled "Deposit of Martyrs" (*Depositio Martyrum*).

The chapel in Kempis's monastery, which had decorations on its ceiling and walls, also had a painted ribbon emblazoned with the three words, "Jesus, Mary, Agnes." According to Farmer, "With other virgin martyrs she . . . appears fairly frequently in late medieval stained glass." (7) Perhaps the monastery of St. Agnes had just such a window. — W.G.

18

Neighboring

What you've done for one of my crowd,
even the lowest of the low,
you've done for me, and indeed to me.

(Matthew 25:40)

Please note the following words: *When you meet a mystery, make the sign of the cross. When you encounter a virtue in another, initiate it.*

Some monastery shop talk. A list of "he whos" and what they mean in spiritual terms.

He who offers a helping hand to a brother in need — it's like taking Jesus by the hand.

He who patiently bears up under the burden imposed on him — it's like carrying Jesus and his crucifix on his own shoulders.

He who reaches out to a deeply saddened brother with comforting words — it's like a lingering kiss on the master's cheek.

He who takes on the fault of another and seeks forgiveness for him — it's like washing and drying the feet of Jesus.

He who restores peace to an angry brother — it's like preparing a bed full of flowers for Jesus.

He who assigns a brother to a higher place at table than himself — it's like feeding Jesus with banquet-sized portions of charity and honeycomb.

He who takes up good meditation on God — it's like introducing Jesus to the inner regions of his heart.

He who brings a book of the Scriptures to a brother — it's like pouring not the house wine, but the best wine, for Jesus.

He who bans jokes from being told at the table — it's like driving mice from the hall where Jesus eats.

He who refuses to listen to baseless detractions or unfounded rumors — it's like taking a big stick and beating a bad dog out of Jesus's house.

He who reads aloud from the Sacred Books while others dine — it's like adding a sparkle to the celestial cup being passed around to Jesus and his dinner companions.

He who reads badly in the refectory certainly doesn't enhance the dining experience, and he who often gets tipsy and tosses — it's like Jesus using his napkin to mop up after.

He who hears of the sins of another and tries to make up the spiritual loss — it's like touching the sacred wounds of Jesus and anointing them.

He who tells the good words and deeds of his neighbor — it's like presenting a bouquet of flowers to Jesus.

He who devoutly reads the words of Jesus and makes them known to others — it's like spreading sweet aromas in the nostrils of Jesus's audience.

He who piously puts up with the defects of another and even excuses them — it's like putting in a plea for mercy from Jesus.

He who refuses to broadcast the scandalous behavior of his neighbor — it's like covering the naked limbs of Jesus.

He who seriously thinks and sweetly ruminates on the divine miracles and the lowly acts of Christ — it's like drinking milk and honey with Jesus. That's what the beatific Agnes said; she shed her own blood for the love of Jesus.

He who reads or sings for a bedridden brother — it's like serenading the baby Jesus in his cradle.

He who prays devoutly, abstains from delicacies, renounces his own property — it's like adding a gift to the Magi's offerings.

He who washes the hats and clothes of his brothers — it's like baptizing Jesus with John the Baptist.

He who keeps to his own cell and observes silence — it's like entering the desert with Jesus.

He who resists vice and castigates his body — it's like fasting with Jesus.

He who says a salutary word to his brother — it's like preaching the kingdom of God with Jesus.

He who faithfully prays for the infirm and the tempted — it's like visiting Lazarus with Jesus, and mourning with Mary and Martha.

He who celebrates Masses for the faithful departed and reads nocturnal prayers for the deceased — it's like rolling the stone with Jesus from the mouth of Lazarus's grave.

He who makes his way with his brothers to a common refectory in order to hear the Holy Book — it's like drinking and dining in the upper room with Jesus and his disciples.

He who stores in his heart the sayings of God as they are read at table — it's like reclining at dinner and putting one's head on Jesus's breast the way John the apostle did.

He who obeys humbly and promptly even in hard times — it's like following Jesus with his disciples to Mount Olivet where he was handed over and taken captive.

He who prays instantly and fervently when he finds himself in trials and tribs — it's like being with Jesus in his agony as he does battle with the devil.

He who totally leaves behind his likes and dislikes — it's like being with Jesus as he carried the cross to Calvary.

He who prays for his adversaries and yet is patient with sinners — it's like being with Jesus as he prays for his enemies lest they perish from their evil ways.

He who spontaneously consigns all his property to God-knows-where — it's like dying on the cross with Jesus or being snatched into paradise with Paul.

He who keeps his heart neat and clean — it's like wrapping the body of Jesus in a fresh shroud and burying it in his heart.

He who perseveres in the service of Jesus all the way to the end — it's like napping with Jesus in the sepulcher.

He who feels the pains of the blessed virgin Mary — it's like consoling her on the loss of her son Jesus who'd never done anything wrong.

He who recalls to mind all the words and deeds of Jesus and breaks them down into their constituent parts — it's like preparing embalming spices that give so much help and solace to the sad and grieving soul.

He who gives humble and devout thanks for all the wonderful things that have happened to him — it's like being with Mary Magdalen on her way to the tomb of Jesus with an apron full of aromatics.

He who makes a firm purpose of amendment after confessing his sins and offering true contrition — it's something like rising with Jesus from the death that is sin.

He who shakes off a dull mind and seizes a new spirit — it's like celebrating a new pasch with Jesus and singing an alleluia with him!

He who turns his back on all the joys of the world, flees all its perils, seeks the religious life, and is allowed entrance — it's like entering the upper room with Jesus and his disciples.

He who turns his back on all temporal things and is totally consumed in holy meditation on celestial things — it's like hanging in there with Jesus and ascending with him to heaven.

As Paul put it in his jailhouse letter to the Philippians, "To live and die with Christ — who can ask for anything more?" (1:21).

He who dies to self — it's like living with Christ.

He who leaves all his perishables — it's like finding that Christ is suited to his taste.

Yes, there's hard labor in leaving the stuff and, yes, there's pain in the dying to self — it's like eternal life with Christ happily reigning.

O when will it be that God is totally mine and I am totally his?

As long as my faithful soul isn't united to God in glory, it can't be full of beatitude.

The conclusion?

He who follows in the fervent footsteps of Christ — it's like having a face-to-face vision with the angels.

Jesus Christ thought it worth his while to lead us after death; he did it for all of us simply by carrying his cross to the bitter end. Amen.

~~~~~~~

DEVOTION TO ST. AGNES

In his works of spirituality, Kempis's prose style is simple enough; metaphors are few and far between; when one appears, it's more the Scripture writer's metaphor than his own. But in his writings about St. Agnes, he produced rich rhetorical prose, flamboyant, over the top, bombastic, extravagant language. His poems and prayers to her seem like love letters. His references to her are lush, love-starved, and they probably popped a few eyes among the novices he was addressing.

In particular I refer to two sermons he delivered on the occasion of the birthday of St. Agnes, presumed to be January 28.

In the first, entitled "Designer Apparel for St. Agnes, Martyr" (De tribus speciosis vestimentis sanctissimae Agnetis virginis), Kempis described her virtues as though they were articles of clothing. According to him she's wearing a white ankle-length tunic signifying purity and virginity. Over that she layers a red or purple garment sprinkled with white flowers signifying patience and martyrdom. Swagged around her waist is a gold silk sash, decorated with milky pearls and blinking gems, signifying charity (VI, 26; 239–48).

His second sermon, titled "Designer Millinery for St. Agnes Virgin" (De aurea corona in capite sanctissimae Agnetis virginis), included prayers to her and accounts of seven miracles attributed to her (VI, 27, 248–81). In five of these cases her help had been fervently implored, but in the last two, a severe flame-up in the chapel and a horse stolen from the stable, no one had implored her help. "The good canons, and especially à Kempis," wrote Vincent Scully in his *Life of the Venerable Thomas à Kempis, Canon Regular of St. Augustine,* "were wont to attribute to the intercession of the girl martyr any notable marks they received [as] the favor of heaven" (241).

Prayer at the end of the sermon. "Agnes, *beatissima, sanctissima,* we've experienced your patronage and protection many times in the past. And so is it any wonder that we devoutly invoke Christ, and properly thank God for all of his good works, many of which have fallen to us because of you. Amen" (281).

Kempis wrote three hymn lyrics in decent rhyming verse. "The Five Joys of Blessed Agnes Virgin" (*Quinque Gaudia Beatae Agnetis Virginis*) and "Rejoice, Agnes, Virgin of Christ" (*Gaude, Agnes, virgo Christi*), which celebrate her virginity, her meek-and-mildness, her gemlike chastity, her to-die-for countenance, and her garden of roses (virtues) (IV, #94, 381–82); and "Hymn of Saint Agnes Virgin" (*Agnetis, Christi Virginis*) (IV, #95, 382–83). —W.G.

19

Praising

Nothing but praise for him.
(Psalm 33:2)

Sweet is the voice the devouts hear now! Sweeter still it will be in the presence of God and the holy angels.

If all the organs play but sound not the praise of God, they huff and puff in vain; that's to say, they don't refresh and satisfy the holy soul.

The honor of God should be the cause of all chanting; no *top twenty pops* here if the praise to God is going to be pleasing and acceptable.

If your intention's pure, then your spirit, as Mary's once did in the joy of her heart, and as Luke recorded it in his gospel, "leaps" (1:47).

A sweet symphony in heaven and earth: a proud choir praising God with pure heart and one voice; with his immense goodness and excellent magnificence as audience.

Praising God is a delightful chore; loving the creator of heaven and earth is entirely appropriate, especially for the unexpected gift of eternal life.

If the lives of the holy angels are spent praising God from the bottom of their beings, why shouldn't ours be as well? I mean, who would get tired of that? But this is precisely how the angels spend their time. Of course they're not weighed down with bodies as we are, nor are they subject to being tripped up by the devils' thingamajigs.

We should recall how as children we sailed through our early lives, avoiding every trial and tribulation. And as adults we should look forward to our next life, where all our laments will be turned into canticles of joy. How beautiful that far-off country where the peaceable kingdom is! No tears of sadness, just tears of joy, full of divine praise and sweet song.

Therefore, faithful soul, bless the Lord of the heavens; the psalmist did it, weighed down as he was in a body, and so can we. "Praise the Lord, Jerusalem; Sion, praise your God" (VUL and NRSV:147:12).

Invoke Jesus on the battlefield, and the Holy Angels will come to your aid, flocking to you from both flanks.

Pray that the hard-hearted demons won't prevail; after all their chiefest weapon is the warm fuzzy, the silken sheet, the down pillow. Don't let the rigor of the order of the day break your spirit. Don't let the manual labor wear you down.

Welcome the holy cross. It's such a burden, yes, but it's also the key to the gate of the heavenly kingdom. What more could you want?

The royal road leading to Christ is conquering one's own will. Put up with your defects; don't let them get you down; just don't sit on a soft cushion all the time, and don't pad your kneeler if your knees will bear you up.

What a deal! A short stint in the vineyard here on earth, and you'll be rewarded with eternal rest and recreation. For your spiritual anonymity and indeed invisibility here on earth you will be singled out for special honor in the next.

Mouth the praise of God always, in good times and bad; just doing this will merit you much if you resign yourself fully to the will of God.

Whatever *gravitas* should come your way interiorly or exteriorly, accept piously and graciously as coming from the hand of the benign Creator who takes care of all of us, that's to say, the important among us as well as the not-so-important.

He made you in his own image, but he seems to have forgotten you. Look around you for what you need; he didn't leave you without the spiritual necessities. Yes, he's that good!

Therefore, open your mouth in praise of the omnipotent God, whose providential actions regulate all the things in heaven and earth, and that would include the sea, the caverns, and cavities of the earth.

Yes, the creator deserves praise. Not to put too fine a line on it, but he made you a human instead of an animal. After all, if he'd made you a fly or a flea, he'd still deserve praise for a fine piece of work! A lion can't boast about his bravery when battling the fly or the flea, the mite or the midge. Just because he can roar louder, that doesn't mean he can make a fly flee or a flea fly.

Lest dissension rise between the high and the low, the rich and the poor, the strong and the weak, the ruling class and the serving class, all of them should praise the Lord. He created every creature; no two alike; incredible variety with irresistible beauty. And, I must admit, human beings have rendered themselves remarkably useful from time to time.

Faithful soul, praise your redeemer. He ransomed you from the hand of eternal death with the passion of his holy cross. There's no way you can repay that, even if you were to be crucified a thousand times.

Praise your protector, who has guarded you against so many dangers and sins. Praise your benefactor who gave you so many gifts, more than you could possibly use, more than you could possibly count.

Even this very day you're still on the receiving list for his new round of gifts. Through his efforts he comes to you on the altar; the ultimate gift in the guise of communion. For this he doesn't require anything from you except your thanks and praise.

When you're happy and are doing fairly well for yourself, pause and give him thanks praise. After all, the pious Lord felt you were worth consoling, worth a nudge in the right direction lest you lose your way.

So many times he's sent bread from heaven to revive your sagging spirit. Just as many times you've read and heard the word of God and devoutly meditated on the incarnation and passion of Christ.

When you're sad or run down, praise and give thanks to God; after all, he visits you, diagnoses you, purges you lest you take for granted the prideful things you'd said about yourself. Bodily affliction often comes from, and indeed is caused by, compunction of the heart.

When you're strong and healthy, praise and give thanks to God; over and over again he's given you the strength to labor for others, with no leisure time for yourself.

When you're in the garden or the orchard, count the different species and name the different trees; smell the flowers, especially the roses; taste the fruits, especially the pears; pinch the herbs, especially the thyme; get a whiff of the lilies. For all these give thanks and praise to God; so many of his marvels growing from the ground. He renews them every year, reflecting his continuing power and wisdom, yes, but also his unflagging desire to provide humankind with pleasures and provisions.

Therefore, in every place and time, give thanks and praise to God. The world is full of his majesty and, as the psalmist put it, "full of his glory above the heavens" (VUL 112:4; NRSV 113:4).

Give thanks and praise to God with all his saints on earth. Do that, and you'll be likened to the angels. If you don't give thanks or praise, you're ungrateful beasts and deserve to eat with the animals!

Behold, birds sing, fish swim, dogs bark, pigs grunt, and all these find ways to praise God. They demonstrate the magnificence of the creator in the movements of the natural world. If they can do it, so can you.

To sum up, never lose sight of God; don't step on your neighbor's toes; give thanks for favors rendered.

Concluding this little book, which was a lot of work, I feel I have to ingratiate myself with God again.

I give thanks and praise to God now and forever. May every other sprite and spirit do the same.

Amen.

THUS ENDS

GARDEN OF ROSES

Valley
of Lilies

Prolog

The just will sprout as lilies;
they'll flower in eternity before the Lord.

(VUL Osee, 14:6; NRSV Hosea 14:5)

My preceding book dealt with the virtues as though they were red roses in a small plot tended by Jesus himself. I hesitated before calling it *A Patch of Roses Somewhere in the Valley of Tears.* This present book speaks again of the virtues but describes them as though they were white lilies. I haven't hesitated to call it *Valley of Lilies.*

Planted in the valley of humility by the Divine Gardener himself, these flowery white trumpets wavering in the wind are gently sprayed by the Holy Spirit.

However, according to Blessed Gregory, the devout who puts together posies of forget-me-nots but forgets to include humility throws beauty to the wind.

Here's what the Canticle of Canticles (NRSV Song of Solomon) has to say about lilies. The humble spouse sings from her mouth and rejoices in her heart about Christ's coming and the gifts he brings.

"My beloved speaks to me, and I to him as we lounge among the lilies" (VUL 6:2; NRSV 6:3).

"My beloved, white from too little sun and red from too much sun" (VUL 5:10; NRSV 5:10) "will linger between my breasts" (VUL 1:12; NRSV 1:13).

To whom be praise, honor, and glory for ever and ever. Amen.

1

Working in the Garden

I'm a flower of the field,
a lily of the valley.

(VUL Canticle of Canticles 2:1; NRSV Song of Solomon 2:1)

Christ is the handsome dashing spouse of Holy Church. He's the head of all the faithful, the flower of all the virtues, the lily of the valley, the lover of humility and chastity.

This book is Christ's voice speaking to his Holy Church in general, and in particular to a certain devout soul.

No need to beat around the bush.

The devout who wants to serve Christ and please the heavenly spouse should make it his aim to conquer his vices, to study and write books whose pages can be turned by hand, to pray frequently and spend his leisure time with God. He should flee the craziness of crowds and relish their secret rendezvous. He shouldn't express opinions about things that don't concern him, nor should he be upset about things injurious to his own reputation.

In God's presence, valor without virtue has little value. A vase may be covered with ornamentation on the outside, but on the inside it's empty as can be. But when it's full of good wine, a pleasant aroma arises from within. That's the way it is with a devout. From his good heart arises good words and holy deeds resulting in great praise for God above and some helpfulness to his neighbor next door.

Therefore, my dear devout, give yourself a good going over. Inventory your virtues. Watch where you stand and how you walk among humankind. Strive to please God with real praise. Build up confidence in others with your holy deeds and habits. Do know that whatever good you do in this regard will redound to the plus side of your record; whatever bad, on the minus side.

Therefore, whenever you eat or drink, sleep or dream, and wherever you spend your leisure time, just know that you're doing the works of the flesh. That's to say, you're carrying on like hairy beasts, roaming, grazing, refreshing themselves in the local streams. They eat and drink their fill and no more. But if anyone gets in their way, they gore the air with their horns and paw the ground with their hooves; their expressionless faces turn to terror, they grind their teeth and they roar in anger, ready to charge.

So much for the beastly side of beasts. But what about the beastly side of human beings? They can be beastly all right, especially when they're gluttonous, avaricious, puffed up with pride, bloated with acrimony, crawling with litigation. Why? They don't have the Spirit of God; they pursue their own passions; they chase after their own tails.

Watch and pray, read and sing, the psalms and hymns about God and his holy people. Fast and abstain from vices and go to the aid of your neighbor. Come to grips with your own sins, confessing and seeking forgiveness. Then and only then are you doing the works of the Holy Spirit. Then you're walking according to the Spirit. Then you're serving the order of the religious life.

It's at times like these that you can be mistaken for holy angels in heaven, always praising and singing and blessing God, never turning their faces away from his.

But when you rejoice at the misfortunes of some or weep at the good fortunes of others, when you look down your nose at your neighbor or seek your own convenience in every messy situation — then it is that you're dressing up like demons and following the rat catcher out of town and down the road, passing through the hamlets of malice and vice.

Make no mistake about it. You're adopting their passions and their brands of wickednesses. They're not good people. They revel in evil. They're trying to seduce and pervert everyone they meet.

The life of the just? It's like that of the angels. The life of the flesh? It's no better than that of the beasts. The life of the proud? Well, it compares well with that of the demons.

Take care. Watch your step. Serve God, not them. He's merciful; they have no mercy. Fall into one of their traps, and they'll just sit and watch you bleed to death, accusing you and confounding you with their accusations.

GOD IN THE GARDEN

The Divine has done some of his best work in one garden or another. Here two Bible dictionaries tell where. Please pardon where the one overlaps the other.

Revell Bible Dictionary

Peoples from Mesopotamia to Egypt viewed gardens as places to relax in and enjoy. The privacy afforded by high walls or thick hedges, the rich smell of growing things, and the tastes of fresh fruits were valued by all peoples of Bible lands. Gardens served as outdoor living areas in the summer, as places for banqueting, even as locations to build shelters where the owner might sleep at night. The author of Ecclesiastes "made gardens and parks and planted all kinds of fruit trees in them" (2:5). The Song of Solomon poetically describes the beloved as a locked garden, filled with choice fruits and spices (4:12–16).

Three gardens play prominent roles in Sacred History.

(1) Adam was placed in the park like Garden of Eden (Genesis 2, 3). There he and Eve were united, disobeyed God, and were exiled from this paradise.

(2) The night before his crucifixion Jesus prayed in Gethsemane, a garden planted with olive trees (Matthew 26:36–46). Here Jesus expressed his anguish and his full submission to the Father's will.

(3) Christ's resurrection took place from a garden tomb (John 19:41). It was a common practice for the rich, such as Joseph of Arimathea in whose tomb the body of Christ was placed, to lay out a garden just outside their last resting place.

Throughout human history, the garden has symbolized a place of beauty, peace, and rest. Thus, the significance of the garden made it an appropriate image of the blessing promised the righteous, who are destined to be "like a well-watered garden, like a spring whose waters never fail" (Isaiah 58:11; compare 51:3; Jeremiah 31:12).

Furthermore, the garden image is used eschatologically in describing the eternal bliss of the righteous. Revelation 22:1–6 describes God's heavenly kingdom in terms of a garden, and just as earthly gardens offer a sanctuary of rest, so God's heaven will provide a place of peace and rest for believers. In heaven, the lost paradise of Eden will be restored (420).

Harper Collins Bible Dictionary

GARDEN, a plot of cultivated land enclosed by walls made of stones, mud brick, or hedges. Entrance was normally through a gate which could be locked (Song of Solomon 4:12; 2 Kings 25:4). Located near ample supplies of water, gardens were lush and desirable pieces of property used both for decorative and utilitarian purposes (Genesis 13:10; Numbers 24:6; Jeremiah 31:12).

Vegetables, spices, fruit trees, and flowers were grown in them (1 Kings 21:2; Jeremiah 29:5; Song of Solomon 4:12–16; Luke 13:19). Gardens were also used as meeting places for social occasions and for meditation and prayer (Esther 1:5; John 18:1).

Occasionally, idolatrous religious practices were carried on in gardens (Isaiah 65:3; 66:17).

Ancestral tombs were often located in gardens. Thus, many Judean kings were buried in garden tombs (2 Kings 21:18, 26), and the body of Jesus was placed to rest in a garden tomb belonging to Joseph of Arimathea (John 19:41–42).

The care of gardens might require the employ of a gardener (John 20:15).

The word "garden" is also used metaphorically and symbolically in the Bible. Thus, in the Song of Solomon, the word refers

to the young woman or bride whom the lover comes to court
(Song of Solomon 4:12; 5:1; 6:2).

Elsewhere, the word refers to the mythical "garden of God" where God walked among the trees in the cool of the day and from which the primordial human beings were banished *(Genesis 2:15; 3:1–3, 8, 10, 23, 24; Ezechiel 28:13; 31:8–9)*. (363) — W.G.

2

Praising God in Poverty

The pauper and the pooper?
They both praise God.

(Psalm VUL 73:21; NRSV 74:21)

Arid, frigid, turgid — we all feel like that from time to time in our prayer life. What to do about it? First, don't despair, come in off the ledge. Second, pray to Jesus as though there's nothing different; keep on praising and giving thanks. And read on in the Holy Books until you find a versicle that seems to speak to you.

"The pauper and the pooper will praise Your name, O Lord."

Many holy and devout who have preceded us have also had such bouts. They've felt left behind by God for a long time. But he had his reasons; among them, that they learn patience with themselves and sufferance with others.

What do I have to say about this? This monastic desert fever, if I may call it that, teaches those who have a life of prayer to keep on an even keel, not to get jumpy in consolation or antsy in desolation.

Reading also helps; something like the following verse by the psalmist. "I'm a beggar and a pauper, but everything's okay; the Lord has taken an interest in my case."

Yes, I put my case in his hands, but is that so bad? He's my strength, my salvation.

The simple truth we have to keep before us at all times is that every good thing comes from God. From that two things follow. First, don't presume that consolation will go on forever. Second, don't expect that desolation will never end.

Whether you're soaring to the heights or sinking to the depths, God is pleased with your prayer. Hence, you needn't plot your daily progress on a wall chart. Be of good cheer. You're going in the right direction.

In and of yourself, you know, you're not worth a whisker. The whole kit and caboodle comes from God.

When the grace of God is given, the sun shines in its heaven, and the soul is illumined from within; that's physical consolation. But when that grace is suddenly snatched from you, then you may truly describe yourself as down and out. Chief symptoms? You're too tired to move, too tired to pray. My advice is, accept desolation as a gift from God. Why? Because he humbles people like you, as he did the elect who've passed before you.

You're one of his special children and from to time, to remind you of the daily discipline, he takes the rod to your back. It's for your many hidden excesses and daily negligences that you may get rid of your pretensions and never think of yourself as a wisdom figure again. That's what the holy Paul advised the Romans. "If you hold your nose in the air, you won't see the trap door on the floor" (11:20).

The soul is doing just fine when it considers itself a thingu-majig, a whatchamacallit, when compared to the rest of God's creation.

JESUS IN THE GARDEN

A favorite getaway for Jesus and his disciples was Mount Olivet, a hill overlooking Jerusalem. It was covered with olive groves, and the scent of olives hung in the air. Part of it, a garden spot, was Gethsemane, the Hebrew word for "olive press." And in the garden there was a structure, perhaps a gazebo (see Luke 22:39–40 and John 18:1). It was at the end of Jesus' last full day on earth; he took them there and said a few words to them, his closest friends. Here's how Matthew described it. Here also is the perfect medieval meditation.

Matthew 26:36–56

"Stay here, would you please? I'm just going off to say a few prayers."

He picked Peter and the two Zebedees, James and John, to accompany him a short distance. Then he sat them down and went a few steps farther. When he began to pray, a great sadness and anxiety came over him. After a while, all upset, he returned to the three lads.

"I'm so sad. Death is coming to visit. Just your sitting here is a help. Watch with me. I need to pray again."

He went off again, but not that far away, and fell on his face.

"Father mine, let me off the hook, if it's at all possible. But who am I to say? Don't listen to me. I'm the one who should be listening to you."

He returned to the lads, but they were sound asleep.

"Peter, you bum, couldn't you have watched an hour with me? Was that too much to ask?"

"Watch and pray," he said to James and John. "Don't let your guard down. Temptation is always ready to steal in. Yes, I know, the spirit is willing, but all flesh is flab."

A second time Jesus went off a few yards and said the same prayer.

"Father mine, let this chalice pass; of course, you know, if I have to take a sip, I will."

He returned to the lads and found the three of them snoring. As for their eyelids, they were sealed tight with fatigue.

He left them a third time, and for a third time he made the same sorry prayer.

When he returned to the lads, he didn't wake them.

"Sleep on. Get the rest you need. As for me, no time to rest now. My time has come. The Son of Man will be handed over to the sinners. Wake up. Let's get out of here. The one who'll hand me over is already in sight."

It was Judas, one of his twelve originals. Following him was a crowd with swords and clubs; they'd been sent by the high priests and elders of the people. All they were waiting for was a signal from Judas, who'd told them, "The one I kiss, he's the one, put him under arrest."

"Greetings, rabbi, what are you doing out here in the middle of the night?" asked Judas as he gave Jesus a kiss.

"Friend, why have you come?"

Then the crowd surged forward, grabbed him, and held him down. But one of his own woke up, grabbed a sword, and started swinging. In the process he cut somebody's ear off; a servant of the high priest's, I think. Immediately Jesus healed the wound.

"Return your sword to its sheath," Jesus said to his lad. "The sword never solved anything, except perhaps dealing death to the sword swinger. Don't you think for a moment that I can't ask my father to intervene! Don't you think he'd send twelve legions of angels if I asked him? But if he did that, the Scriptures wouldn't be fulfilled.

"So, what's the big deal?" asked Jesus, turning his attention to the crowd. "You came out here to arrest me as though I were public enemy number one. You could have grabbed me in the temple any time you wanted; I teach there every day."

All this was done so that the Scriptures of the prophets might be fulfilled.

As Jesus was being lugged off, the rest of the disciples disappeared into the night (Matthew 26:36–56).

Prayer of Thomas à Kempis

Kempis writing on the passion is very much like Paul writing on the passion. Indeed in his "Sermons on the Life and Passion of the Lord," he quotes Paul's now-famous sentiment (#21, III, 178). "I stand in front of you as an expert, and yet I have to admit that I know nothing; the only thing I know is Jesus and him crucified" (1 Corinthians 2:2). Here is a prayer of Kempis's, taken from the same sermon.

Take notice, my soul. Turn your eyes from all the vanities and travesties of the world. Direct your heart instead to Jesus crucified. Stand watch with him through the wee small hours on the Mount of Olives, and pray with him to his Father. The chalice of his blessed passion was given to him to drink. May that same chalice be passed to you, burning with affection to lovingly endure the same. Amen (#21, III, 178–79). —W.G.

3

Putting Souls to the Test

Just in the Lord, rejoice!

(Psalm VUL 32:1; NRSV 33:1)

In heaven joy can always be found. In hell pain can never be avoided. In the world, well, both heaven and hell fight it out for equal time. The reason? To put both the good and the bad to the test.

In summer the days are bright, sometimes too bright. So it is with the devout soul when the grace of God comes and illuminates it; then the things hidden in the nooks and crannies of the soul come into sight and can be recognized and understood; then the soul breaks out in song and jubilation.

In winter the days grow shorter, darker, cooler. It's temptation time when the grace of devotion seems to shrivel. The intellect darkens, the mind trembles.

It's time for the soul to be patient. Funny thing about patience, it's entirely acceptable to the Lord. And patience in adversity, far from being a passive virtue, is a rugged aerobic exercise that toughens the soul, muscles up the virtue one already has. And patience will have its own reward in the next life.

In addition to patience, a few strokes of flagellation inflicted upon one's own shoulders from to time have a remedial effect. Humbling is promoted; pride is confounded; vainglory evanesces.

As long as the soul is in the body, it'll be exercised by both good and bad, which will result in either progress or regress in the love of Christ.

Therefore, the art of exercise may be said to be the virtue of handling both the good and the bad.

Therefore, dear soul, bless the Lord always, in good times as well as bad; praise God your Sion day and night; and your reward will be great in the presence of God in heaven or on earth. Just some thoughts to live by as you endure both prosperity and adversity, goodness and badness, happiness and sadness.

Whence the apostle Paul said, "As for those who love God, the very thing seems to work together toward good" (8:28). Nothing derails those who fear and respect him. Blessed are those who follow the word of God in all things!"

<hr />

PARABLES IN THE GARDEN

"Why do you talk in parables?" asked the disciples.

"Because I have this plan," replied the Lord. "I want you to know the mysteries of the kingdom of heaven, but I don't want them [the scribes and pharisees] to know" (Matthew 13:10–11).

What follows is food for a number of medieval meditations.

Fertile Soil

There was this farmer who didn't know what he was doing. He grabbed a bag of seed and sowed that seed every which way. Some fell on the footpaths; the birds had a nice lunch. Some fell on gravelly ground; sprouts quickly appeared, then perished from lack of nourishment below and too much sun above. Some fell on shrubs where there was a constant battle for sun and food; the thorns eventually choked the grains. Some fell on good soil, and the rest was history; a bumper crop with some acres producing as much as thirtyfold, sixtyfold, even hundredfold. So what does this parable of the mad sower mean? You have ears. You figure it out (Matthew 13:3–9).

Fig Tree

How do you know when spring ends and summer begins? Well, the fig tree knows. When its branches pump up and its buds begin to appear, that's when the happy time begins. That's when the Son of Man will be nearing the garden gates (Matthew 24:32–33).

Grain Seed

So the kingdom of God is like a sower broadcasting his seed; after that he had nothing else to do. But life went on, and the seed germinated and grew. How this happened he didn't have a clue, but we know. The soil did all the work. First the bud, then the stalk, then the beard of the fully grown grain. Then the farmer knew what he had to do; it was harvest time, and he made his sickle do all the work (Mark 4:26–29).

Mustard Seed

So what's the kingdom of God really like? What parable can I cook up that's close? Well, it's like a mustard seed, tiniest of seeds. Put it in the soil, and before you know it, it's grown out of all proportion, a haven for birds who want to nest, a haven for all who want to rest (Mark 4:30–32).

Vines

I'm the true vine, and my father is the real farmer. The vine has to bear fruit; the branch that can't has to be lopped. The branch that can, however, has to be pruned back to produce even more fruit in the future. So what has this got to do with the price of prunes? . . . The vine can't produce without branches; branches can't produce without vines. Yes, I'm the vine and you, the branches. Stay with me, and I'll stay with you; and that should produce no end of fruit (John 15:1–5).

Weeds

The kingdom of heaven is like the farmer who sowed good seed during the day. But that very night while he slept, his mortal enemy came and sowed rye, a wildly successful grass, among the wheat. So when the wheat appeared, so did the rye. Alarmed, the field hands ran to the farmer.

"Master, did you sow wheat or rye?"

"An enemy of mine has done this."

"So what do you want us to do?" asked the field hands, "dig them both up and replant?"

"Do that, and you'll pull the wheat with the rye," replied the farmer. "Let's let them grow to full height and then do the harvest. Then it'll be easier to sort the two. Store the grain, yes, but burn the grass" (Matthew 13:24–30). —W.G.

4

Loving the Silly and the Serious

Love the silly as well as the serious;
after all, he made them both in his own image.

(Psalm VUL 30:24; NRSV 31:23)

The true lover of God loves God truly; that's to say, loves God because of what he is and because of the joy he finds in him. We shouldn't love God because it's convenient for us to do so, nor because he promised solace or reward. We should love him totally and finally because he's worth it and good for it.

So the psalmist frequently, repeatedly, says in the praise of God. "Let's confess to the Lord because he's good; but that's not to say that the Lord doesn't like all this loving. It's just to say that on the other side, when he looks over the penitent's sins, he'll have some sweet words to say" (VUL 105.1; NRSV 106:1).

Therefore, the fragile person shouldn't despair of his sins before he dies. Why? Because the Lord often expresses himself after a human dies, in one's first days in eternity, if eternity may be said to have days.

The person who loves God profoundly, profoundly humbles himself.

Happy the person who puts other people in front of himself and avoids everything known to displease God.

Happy the person who devotes all his work to God. And whatever good thought he thinks, he defers to the praise and honor of God.

Happy the person who retains nothing for himself, and freely returns everything God gave him.

❧❧❧❧❧❧❧❧

COLORS

According to a Parisian tailor of the fifteenth century, gray, black, and violet were quiet favorites with the locals, but at the public festivals loud colors ran riot. Red topped the list; red with blue and blue with violet were favorite combinations. And then there was the lady who wore a violet silk outfit and covered her horse-drawn carriage in blue silk; she was accompanied by three men in vermillion silk doublets with green silk hoods.

Black velvet was favored by royalty. In his later years Philip the Good wore nothing else; his attendants did the same, and his horse was arrayed in the same color. King René, who thought himself a tastemaker, combined black with gray and white.

Blue and green were the colors of love. Blue for fidelity, green for erotic love.

Yellow and brown would dawn in the Renaissance (Huizinga, 270–71).

Who knows what the aspirants wore who came to join the Brothers and Sisters of the Common Life or even the Augustinian priests and sisters on the hill? Whatever, Kempis would tone these postulants and novices down.

As for himself, in *Roses* and *Lilies,* he didn't mention a color, except that roses were red and lilies were white. But was his world, the world he lived in, so bland? Was he himself color-blind?

Such portraits that have survived picture him in the traditional white cassock of the Augustinians. Over that he wore a long surplice with loose sleeves. On his head was a cap or bonnet that in later generations would become a biretta. For winter use there was a sweeping black cape in which a monk could easily be lost in the warmth.

As in the secular realm, these monkish colors weren't just colors; they symbolized the abstract qualities the wearer was striving for. Cassock and surplice of white signified purity of heart and soul; cape of black reflected decay and the death of the things of this world (Scully, *Life of the Venerable Thomas à Kempis,* 112).

So in black and white Kempis could be said to be looking rather smart for a religious. But in his liturgical attire he could look downright colorful! In his time five colors were approved for general use in the Roman Rite.

White. Symbol of light, typified innocence and purity, joy and glory. Proper to Trinity Sunday, feasts of Our Lord except those of his passion, feasts of the Blessed Virgin Mary, angels, men and women who were saints but not martyrs, masses for marriage and burial of children.

Red. Language of fire and blood, indicating charity and martyrs' generous sacrifice. Proper to Pentecost week, feasts of

Christ's passion and precious blood; finding and elevating the Cross; feasts of apostles and martyrs.

Green. Plants and trees, bespeaking the hope of life eternal. Proper to time from end of epiphany to beginning of lent and from pentecost to advent.

Violet. Gloomy cast of the mortified, denoting affliction and melancholy. Proper during advent and lent.

Black. Universal emblem of mourning, signifying the sorrow of death and the somberness of the tomb. Proper to masses for the dead and on Good Friday.

Additional colors. Rose for *Gaudete* Sunday and *Laetare* Sundays, bright spots during the gloom of advent and lent respectively. Blue in some dioceses in Spain for the mass in honor of the Immaculate Conception (*Catholic Encyclopedia*, 4:134–45).

Each day had its color, and it would be found in the altar antependium and the tabernacle veil; the burse and chalice veil; and the maniple, stole, chasuble, cope, and humeral veil of the celebrant; maniple, stole, tunic, and dalmatic of the assisting ministers.

So Kempis, the quiet man, the ascetical man, found himself daily swanning around during the liturgy in a chapel with decorated walls and ceilings. He was anything but bland. In fact, he was as splendidly turned out as the best of his age.

How does that compare with his insistence that all flesh is grass? All flash, a puff of smoke?

What are we of the twenty-first century to think when Kempis spent half of his day condemning the puffery of the world, and the other half approving that same puffery in the praise and joy of the Lord? To listen to or read Kempis, one would think he found colors corrosive.

Perhaps a modern meditation is in order. Is color a spiritual nicety or a spiritual necessity in the twenty-first century?

—W.G.

5

Thanking for
Every Good Thing

Come magnify the Lord with me,
and we'll exalt his name together.

(Psalm VUL 33:4; NRSV 34:3)

Be thankful for small favors; small thanks often turn into great praise.

Don't devalue God's gifts and favors simply because he doesn't require thanks up front. They really do come with no strings attached.

No, God doesn't seek or require anything in return. Every now and then a nod from you would be nice. Nicer still would be sinning no more. Nicest of all would be showing God you'll never forget his generosity; no, not even for a minute.

The sort of person God will single out in heaven is the one who always put God ahead of himself, thought himself unworthy of God's attention, didn't get infatuated with earthly good or infuriated with earthly bad.

Will there be people who'll deserve more heavenly recognition? Yes, people like Job, whose golden reputation was ruined by others and whose property was snatched. Nevertheless, he gave thanks, rejoiced, felt blessed as though nothing were wrong. In place of his conspicuous wealth came nothing but trash and exile and uncertainty about what hideous thing would come next — all this loss he counted as spiritual gain, he kept his chin up and stopped complaining. Well, not right away, but in the end.

Happy the person who welcomes the rod of pain as piously as the hand of God, and totally offers and commits himself to the divine will.

Happy the person who seeks what really tickles God's fancy and does it.

Happy the person who welcomes yesterday's food as though it were today's, remains merry though mauled for life, considers hell-on-earth still something of an advantage for the soul.

6

Conforming with the Cross

I'm with him in times of trouble.

(Psalm VUL 90:15; NRSV 91:15)

So, Lord, asked the disciple, what does this quote, this lily, this versicle mean? There's a sweet something in it for me, but I just don't know what it is.

Yes, my child, replied the Lord, but there's more than one meaning, as you'll find in this series of "when you's."

When you are in the middle of troubs and tribs, and your chest aches, you wonder where you are. Well, one place you are, although you may not know it, is with Jesus on the cross.

When you experience consolation and rejoice with hymns and canticles, then you're rising from the dead with Jesus, mouthing joyful alleluias.

When you pray for your sins on bended knees and really express sorrow for them, then, though you may not realize it at the time, you're knocking with heavy fists on the door of heaven.

When you turn your meditation from earthly stuff to heavenly stuff, then, though you may not know it, you're heading toward heaven with Jesus in hand and accompanied by oodles of angels.

Therefore, the only sensible thing to do is be meek and mild, humble and patient, in every situation. Put God over self. Carry your cross today the way Jesus did then. That's to say, every affliction of the flesh patiently tolerated is medicine for the soul, satisfaction for sins, and hope of future beatitude. Amen.

ᔕᕀᔕᕀᔕᕀᔕᕀᔕᕀᔕᕀᔕ

PROVERBS

Kempis was a master of the proverb as a purveyor of spiritual knowledge and instruction; each of his major works contains hundreds of them. Here's what Huizinga had to say about the use of proverbs outside the monastery.

In the thought of the Middle Ages proverbs have performed a very living function. There were hundreds in current use in every nation. The greater number are striking and concise. Their tone is often ironical, their accent always that of bonhomie and resignation. The wisdom we glean from them is sometimes profound and beneficent. They never preach resistance.

The big fishes eat the smaller!
The badly dressed are placed with their back to the wind!
None is chaste if he has no business!
At need we let the devil help us!
No horse is so well shod that he never slips!

To the laments of moralists about the depravity of man the proverbs oppose a smiling detachment. The proverb always glazes over iniquity. Now it is naively pagan and almost evangelical. A people which has many proverbs in current use will be less given to talking nonsense, and so will avoid many confused arguments and empty phrases. Leaving arguments to cultured people, it is content with judging each case by referring to the authority of some proverb. The crystallization of thought in proverbs is therefore not without advantage to society.

Proverbs in their crude simplicity were thoroughly in accordance with the general spirit of the literature of the epoch. The level reached by authors was but little higher than that of the proverbs. . . .

In political speeches and in sermons, proverbs are in frequent use. . . .

He who is silent about all things is troubled by nothing!

A well-groomed head wears the helmet badly!

He who serves the common weal is paid by none for his trouble! (229–31). —W.G.

7

Walking
with the Pure Soul

Let's walk while we still have the light.

(John 12:35)

Who walks with God in the lingering light? The person who wants nothing in this world, who has his heart fixed on God in the next.

For the ambulatory soul, the Lord Jesus Christ is a buried treasure, containing all sorts of good stuff.

The person who doesn't have God for a friend is a mess; he has a lot of possessions, but he's clouded his own mind into thinking he needs them all.

He who has God for a friend loves him and does what he says, at least according to the evangelist John (14:23).

He who keeps the word of God never spouts a casual word. He does what he said he'd do; he doesn't blow his own horn; he spots the good in others and decides to do the same. He refers all glory back to God.

He who's out to please himself has a dummkopf to please.

So in all you do and say, make pleasing God your topmost priority. That'll result in his keeping you at the top of his list.

Why do you mess around so much with the goods of this world? After all you're only a mortal, soon to be a morsel enjoyed by the worms.

You may be young, a lad, a junior person, but that's no excuse. The goods of this world are twitching your thread this way and that. Everybody can see that except you. So it's time for you to listen to an old fox, a senior person like myself. That's not the way to find rest in the spiritual life. You have to turn your heart around. You have to focus on God. You have to make a good friend out of him.

8

Speaking Nonstop with God

God's place, located in charming rural surroundings.

(Psalm VUL 75:3; NRSV 76:2)

Who's got peace? Why, the person who's meek and mild in heart!

Why do you stick your nose into the affairs of others when you're neglecting your own spiritual progress?

The person who humbles himself and sweats it out because of God has more peace than he knows what to do with. Because he has God in his heart, every burden laid on him is light.

Inside the monastery, by praying and meditating, singing and reading, the monk speaks nonstop with God. As for the stuff that goes on outside the monastery, well, there's not a lot to say.

Three *wherevers*. Wherever you are, wherever you came from, wherever you're going to, your thoughts go with you.

By their effects you will know them, and here's a list.

Good meditation has a positive effect; bad meditation, a negative effect.

Anger has a disturbing effect; envy, a blinding effect; hatred, a destructive effect.

Holy reading has an educational effect; prayer, an elevating effect; exercise, a fulfilling effect.

Holy conversation has a cleansing effect; silly conversation, a sniggering effect; leisurely chitchat, a scandalizing effect.

Heavy conversation has a dulling effect; pious conversation, a delightful effect; moral conversation, an edifying effect.

Historical conversation has a confirming effect; celestial conversation, an ethereal effect.

Summing up the effects, cleanse your soul of every malice, and you'll never scratch again.

There's no good peace to be found by the virtuous except in God.

Two *helps*. Silence helps, and long-suffering helps.

Eventually, God will liberate you from every burden, great and small.

A happy life and a good conscience are deposits in the bank when it comes to death and dying; a bad conscience makes for a fearful and stressful death.

The angry person stumbles from one sin to another.

By praying for an enemy, the meek and mild make a friend out of him. That's just the sort of thing that pleases God!

LILIES IN SCRIPTURE

In *Lilies* Kempis relies heavily on the reader's having a rather extensive knowledge of the lilies found in Scripture. Hence the following helpful entry from the *Harper Bible Dictionary*.

LILY, a flower such as the hyacinth or tulip that grows from a bulb (true lily). Similar groups include the iris, crocus, and narcissus.

The reference to "lilies of the field" in Matthew (6:28–30) and Luke (12:27–28) implies an impressive showing of blossoms and variety of colors and therefore may be identified as the common crown anemone or windflower (Anemone coronaria). This poppy-like flower, which is not a true lily, blooms brightly and profusely in the spring throughout the hilly country of the Holy Land.

The lilies mentioned in the Song of Solomon (2:1–2 and 5:13) are referred to as symbols of beauty.

The "lily of the valleys" of the Song of Solomon (2:1–2) is not our common lily-of-the-valley, but most likely the sweet-smelling blue hyacinth (Hyacinthus orientalis) common in fields and rocky places.

The lilies gathered in the gardens (Song of Solomon 6:2) may be true lilies such as the distinctive white Madonna lily (Lilium candidum) and the scarlet martagon (Lilium chalcedonicum), both of which are native to the Holy Land. The white Madonna lily is often traditionally depicted in representations of the annunciation as a symbol of the purity of the virgin.

The lilies that form the decorative floral motif of Solomon's Temple (1 Kings 7:19, 26) are probably water lilies or the lotus (genus Nymphaea) This flower is commonly represented in Egyptian architecture as well (608). —W.G.

9

Recollecting the Heart

Help me or harm me — pick one!
(Luke 11:23)

That's what our Lord Jesus Christ said.

When you sowed your wild oats, you fell for the fantasies of the devil and the passions of the heart; that's to say, you lost a lot of spiritual ground. Some of that you may recover in a variety of ways; none of them extravagant.

Attend the Sunday Mass.

Recite the daily Angelus.

Recollect your inner self.

Alone, far from the sight of others, prostrate yourself before the holy cross. An image of the blessed virgin Mary would also be appropriate. Perhaps a pious picture of a saint.

Invoke Jesus with Mary and all the angels and saints.

Pray that mercy and the grace of divine consolation return to you.

Pray with the holy David as in one of his psalms. "Lord, I've laid out my desires for you to see, and my penances haven't been hidden from you" (VUL 37:10; NRSV 38:9).

"Lord, the hope of my youth, when the going gets rough, I flee to you. Encourage me to dump my desires and follow you always" (VUL 142:9–10; NRSV 143:9–10).

That should be pleasing to you and practical for me.

Lord, never let me do any thought, desire, or act that would displease you or hurt others; this is as you've prescribed to me and all the others serving You.

When I do just the opposite of what you ask me to do, correct me on the spot; don't let your anger linger. You're God, and I'm a pauper and pooper who desperately needs your grace and mercy.

May your name be holy now and forever more!

10

Guarding against Temptation

Watch and pray
lest you walk right smack into temptation:
temptations of the flesh, the spirit,
the devil, the world.
(Mark 14:38)

Temptation is fed by various fuels. Flesh feeds the bonfire of concupiscence; spirit, the spitfire of pride; devil, the slow burn of envy; world, the flash fire of vanity.

Christ approaches temptation from just the opposite direction. He persuades you to cultivate chastity, humility, charity, and contempt of the world. Why? To promote the kingdom of God and provide an alternative to the pains of hell.

One must watch and pray. That's because there's no security anywhere against the bad breath of the adversary who never sleeps, never rests.

As Peter put it in his first, the adversary circles round, hunts for prey (5:8); he gets in the way of pious exercises and makes loud noises during prayerful times.

So our Lord Jesus Christ, who factors in the wickedness of the devil and the usefulness of prayer as well as the fortitude of the enemy and the debility of humankind, vigorously admonished his disciples and indeed all the faithful to watch and pray; that's to say, if they don't want to be overrun by the enemy. Don't fall for the foolishness of the devil. Don't cooperate with his crazy schemes.

If you can't read the whole psalter, then pick out a psalm, perhaps an old favorite, and read it again and again. Pick a verse or a hymn about Jesus or Mary or a saint, perhaps a favorite of yours, and mull it over — all this to keep the vigil fires burning. The devil is near but, as the psalmist reminds us, God is nearer; you merely have to call his name (VUL 144:18; NRSV 145:18).

The humble prayer of the just person penetrates the heavens, adds credibility to God, breaks the stranglehold of the devil, gives the lie to his threats.

The evangelist Matthew described it this way. "If your prayer life isn't helped by what happens outside the monastery, then stay home and do what Christ says. Go to your cubicle, shut the door behind you, leaving you and the Father alone. Pray to him" (6:6). He knows what you need.

What to pray? Just say the following or something very much like it.

Father, may your will always be done. Do to me what's pleasing to you and practical for me.

If you're in a chorus with others, read and sing with them as the angels do with Jesus.

Sing out externally, yes, but inwardly grieve for your sins. That'll please humankind, the men and women you meet every day, and it won't displease God and his holy angels.

Odd thing, God pays special attention to the quiet compunction of the heart; the squawks and squeaks of a high voice he pays no attention to.

Humble prayer is what God likes; what he doesn't like is vain glory.

Through waves of tears, grace is acquired and virtue increased; devotion, on the other hand, dies the death through waves of sound.

For every fault and negligence, punishment is rendered.

Against these evils divine piety must always be on guard as it leads the parade to the heavenly kingdom.

~~~~~~~~~~

PRIDE AND GREED

In the present chapter, "Guarding against Temptations," Kempis mentions pride and greed (cupidity) as two characteristics of the eternal soul, and indeed medieval life. Here's what the historian Huizinga had to say about them.

Medieval doctrine found the root of all evil either in the sin of pride or in [greed]. Both opinions were based on Scripture texts.

A superbia initium sumpsit omnis perditio [Every perdition has taken its beginning from pride]; the closest these words come to is a passage in Proverbs, "Pride comes before contrition, and the spirit howls just before it collapses" [16:16].

Radix omnium malorum est cupiditas [The root of all evils is love of money [greed]] [1 Timothy 6:10].

It seems, nevertheless, that from the twelfth century downward people begin to find the principle of evil rather in [greed] than in pride....Pride might perhaps be called the sin of the feudal and hierarchic age.

Very little property is, in the modern sense, liquid, while power is not yet associated, predominantly, with money; it is still rather inherent in the person and depends on a sort of religious awe which he inspires; it makes itself felt by pomp and magnificence, or a numerous train of followers.

Feudal or hierarchic thought expresses the idea of grandeur by visible signs, lending to it a symbolic shape, of homage paid kneeling, of ceremonial reverence. Pride, therefore, is a symbolic sin, and from the fact that, in the last resort, it derives from the pride of Lucifer, the author of all evil, it assumes a metaphysical character.

[Greed], on the other hand, has neither this symbolic character nor these relations with theology. It is a purely worldly sin, the impulse of nature and of the flesh. In the later Middle Ages the conditions of power had been changed by the increased circulation of money, and an illimitable field opened to whosoever was desirous of satisfying his ambitions by heaping up wealth.

To this epoch [greed] becomes the predominant sin. Riches have not acquired the spectral impalpability which capitalism, founded on credit, will give them later; what haunts the imagination is still the yellow tangible gold. The enjoyment of riches is direct and primitive; it is not yet weakened by the mechanism of an automatic and invisible accumulation by investment; the satisfaction of being rich is found either in luxury and dissipation, or in gross avarice.

Toward the end of the Middle Ages feudal and hierarchic pride had lost nothing, as yet, of its vigor; the relish for pomp and display is as strong as ever. This primitive pride has now united itself with the growing sin of [greed], and it is this mixture of the two which gives the expiring Middle Ages a tone of extravagant passion that never appears again.

A furious chorus of invectives against [greed] and avarice rises up everywhere from the literature of that period. Preachers, moralists, satirical writers, chroniclers, and poets speak with one voice. Hatred of rich people, especially of the new rich, who were then very numerous, is general. Official records confirm the most incredible cases of unbridled avidity told by the chronicles.

In 1436 a quarrel between two beggars, in which a few drops of blood had been shed, had soiled the Church of The Innocents in Paris. The bishop, Jacques du Châtelier, "a very ostentatious, grasping man, of a more worldly disposition than his station required," refused to consecrate the church anew unless he received a certain sum of money from the two poor men, which they did not possess, so that the service was interrupted for twenty-two days (27–29). — W.G.

11

Fearing
Eternal Punishment

May fear of God freeze my joints.

(Psalm VUL 118:120; NRSV 119:120)

This prayer is useful in the continuing fight against the vices of the flesh. Not that it's unhelpful when it comes to unseating pride from its unlawful throne in your mind. The flesh always clamors for excitement, and spirit always rises above its station in the vain hope of praise. Together these two vices have continued to vex and harass humankind since the beginning.

Are these sins and, if so, mortal or venial? If not mortal sins, then certainly venial ones.

When wretched flesh, always a-tiptoe on death's doorstep, tempts you, think of the torments of the eternal fire. Snuff the bonfire of concupiscence with the fire of Gehenna. What's the principle here? Major motions drive out minor ones. What's the result? The flaming spirit is saved by the cleansing fire.

Every delectation of the flesh flits by before you know it.

Every worldly enjoyment falls flat, and that would include every embellishment of the body, every honor and glory.

Just as headache forces the dissolute to mourn and weep for their sorry lot, so the fear of death and the heat of hell make the passionate person abstain from sins.

The person who has no fear of sin quickly tumbles into it. And the proud person who doesn't know his lowly station is primed for a drubbing by the devils. That sentence stands firm and true; it doesn't depend on whether the being is human or angelic.

Some wisdom from the letter of James. "God resists the proud but gives grace to the humble" (4:6). An echo of it is found in Peter's first (5:5). Such has been the experience of the saints and the rest of his elect since the beginning.

What's the conclusion? You should have a profound fear of God's judgment when the record of your life is finally reviewed. One thing is sure: you don't want to point out your worldly accomplishments to the reviewer.

Even though you've tried your hardest, your life record is still full of holes; conservatively speaking, your bad deeds outnumber your good deeds by a thousand to one.

You have every right to fear the switch of God, the scourge, the judgment to come; then no bad deed will pass unpunished; no good deed will go unrewarded.

If your room is on fire, doesn't that ignite your fear and bounce you up and out of the room as quickly as you can?

What does the thought of future punishments produce? Fear and trembling?

Sometimes the horror of hell turns out to be a better motivation than tepid prayer, sometimes even than fervent prayer.

12

Using the Lord's Passion as a Weapon

**Blessed are those who mourn,
for they'll be comforted.**

(Matthew VUL 5:5; NRSV 5:4)

They'll be comforted, yes, but by whom? Certainly by Christ in the confines of the heart, but not by the fleshy, flashy people of this world.

Jokes and japes have no place in the consideration of Christ's sacred passion. Frequent outbursts of hilarity put even more sting in Christ's already smarting wounds.

If you were to have one sharp thorn from the crown of Jesus' head stuck in the middle of your back, would you be laughing? I don't think so. And you have a choice. Instead of lying in a bed of thorns, you can weep more, grieve louder, make a terrible fuss about your sins.

If you were to have one nail of the cross driven through your foot, where would you run? Not far. But you don't have to get up and run; you just have to sit and mourn for your past sins more than ever before. That way you get some idea of what Christ went through for you.

Would that I could cry enough bitter tears to buy the remission of all my sins, but I can't! My poor spitting and spouting could never equal the redeeming quality of Christ's holy wounds.

What to do?

When you feel depressed or tempted, quickly turn to prayer, which you can use as a shield against the onslaughts, and to the cross, which you can wave as a signal to the enemy that you're going to fight back. What ails us needs the salvific medicine that is spouting from Christ's holy wounds. Yes, devout prayer and serious remembrance of his passion are our best weapons against the enemy.

Look at Jesus on the cross, no clothes, nailed like a felon, and the pain, the shame, of it all. Yes, we must weigh, muse, wonder at the magnitude, longitude, even altitude of that ghastly and yet ghostly sight.

One thing you can do in contemplation is count the number of sharp thorns stuck in his head and marvel at the blood fountaining from these punctures for us.

Consider these and other images of the passion of Jesus Christ as arms in the war against the enemy. Put them under your pillow where you can reach them day or night. You don't want the devil to find you with no divine images at hand; he'll gladly fill the vacuum with wallets full of sordid pictures of his own.

Remember the holy nativity of our Lord Jesus Christ; it too is another good weapon in the fight against the devils and the dissolutes. Make your bed more like his. A little hay for him, no silk coverlet, some milk from his virgin mother's breast. And for you a pallet, lumpy, not plumped up with feathers and yet full of virtues.

May the hardness of your mattress and the thinness of your pillow help you recall the stone of the sepulcher of our Lord Jesus Christ, truly dead and buried in the heart of the earth and enclosed with a large stone.

Here rest in the peace of God and forget all the things of the world.

Here you can surely see that all the earthly entertainments have no lasting value.

Here rise with him now in virtue and grace, and on the last day with the elect in glory sempiternal. Amen.

MOURNING

In the present chapter, "Using the Lord's Passion as a Weapon," Kempis incited in his audience a sentiment of mourning for past sins just as the medieval population at large was mourning for all sorts of losses. Here's what Huizinga had to say about mourning at large.

The diatribes of the preachers against dissoluteness and luxury produced violent excitement which was translated into action. Long before Savonarola started bonfires of the "vanities" at Florence, to the irreparable loss of art, the custom of these holocausts of articles of luxury and amusement was prevalent both in France and Italy.

At the summons of a famous preacher, men and women would hasten to bring cards, dice, finery, ornaments and burn them with great pomp.

Renunciation of the sin of vanity in this way had taken a fixed and solemn form of public manifestation, in accordance with the tendency of the age to invent a style for everything.

All this general facility of emotions, of tears and spiritual upheavals, must be borne in mind in order to conceive fully how violent and high-strung life was at that period.

Public mourning still presented the outward appearance of a general calamity. At the funeral of Charles VII, the people are quite appalled on seeing the cortège of all the court dignitaries, dressed in the deepest mourning, which was most pitiful to see; and because of the great sorrow and grief they exhibited for the death of their master, many tears were shed and lamentations uttered throughout the town....

Solemnities of a political character also led to abundant weeping. An ambassador of the king of France repeatedly burst into tears while addressing a courteous harangue to Philip the Good....

Unquestionably there is some exaggeration in these descriptions of the chroniclers. In describing the emotion caused by the addresses of the ambassadors at the peace congress of Arras in 1435, Jean Germain, bishop of Chalons, makes the auditors throw themselves on the ground, sobbing and groaning. Things, of course, did not happen thus, but thus the bishop thought fit to represent them, and the palpable exaggeration reveals a foundation of truth (13–15). —W.G.

13

Invoking
Jesus and Mary

***Put me on the straight and narrow,
my Lord and God, and keep me there.***

(Psalm VUL 5:9; NRSV 5:8)

Your highways, Lord, Jesus Christ, are beautiful ways, clean
and secure routes; perfect for walking the walk. All your byways are peaceful and holy, leading the faithful and humble
of heart in a roundabout way to the heavenly kingdom.

Therefore, wherever you're heading, walking, standing, re-
siding, invoke the names of Jesus and his pious mother Mary.
And whenever you need some wisdom for the road, you may
say the following prayer.

*Put me on the straight and narrow, my Lord and God, then
give me a shove.*

To that prayer you can add this one from the psalms.

*"Shadow me closely," Lord Jesus, so that I don't wander off to see
the sights" (VUL 16:5; NRSV 17:5). And monitor my conversation
so that I don't fall into the fashionable small talk.*

After these, try this sweet versicle for your food allowance.
Pray it firmly and devoutly.

May Jesus and Mary be with me always on the journey. In every place, at every time, may they be good guides in case I take the wrong path and start seeing things that can't be right.

This holy prayer is short to read, light to carry, easy to hold, sweet to think about, strong to provide protection, faithful for the watch, good to have as a map, delightful to recreate with, amicable to console, able enough to help, prudent enough to lead every pauper and pooper on the straight and narrow, and every hater of the world to life eternal.

This holy prayer has with it companions and soldiers enough to face all the kings and princes of the world. And it invokes saints higher than one would find in the general population.

This holy prayer draws to itself the whole celestial curia, which follows with all reverence the Lord himself, Jesus Christ, and his lady, holy mother Mary, who's worthy of all praise and honor.

He who has these two companions on the pilgrimage road will find them pious patrons at the moment of death.

Don't desert Jesus, and don't give him the slip if you want to live a joyful life with him and his mother.

A pilgrim carries Jesus and Mary in his heart, utters their names, mouths their blessings, applauds them with his hands, dances with joyful feet, cries with loud voice, rejoices in his heart, mourns with his eyes, placates with kisses, embraces with his arms, and pays his respects on bended knee.

Happy is he who invokes Jesus and Mary seriously, salutes them devoutly, commemorates them lovingly, honors them generously, rejoices with them joyfully, glorifies them highly, loves them ardently, sweet-talks them smoothly, celebrates them exuberantly.

How sweet Jesus is! How sweet his holy mother Mary is!

Happy the pilgrim who on the road carries in his body the memory of his celestial homeland; there Jesus and Mary divide their time with all the angels and saints.

Happy the pilgrim who doesn't seek a big house on earth, but desires to be in the heavenly mansion with Jesus. Happy the pauper and the pooper who don't stop supplicating God at his holy table until he gives each a morsel.

Happy is he who's called to the supper of the lamb; he welcomes the sacrament until he can arrive at the final convivium.

When the faithful communicates devoutly, or the priest celebrates reverently, he may be said to have dined with Jesus and his blessed mother.

Who is a disciple of Jesus, chaplain of blessed Mary virgin, companion of the angels, fellow citizen of the apostles, member of God's family, relative of the saints, friend of heaven?

He's the sort of person who finds no pleasure in crowds, avoids telling tall tales, thinks the way Jesus thinks, keeps serious guard on his heart and other senses lest he offend Jesus and Mary and all the saints. As the psalmist has said, "He will receive benediction and mercy from the Lord" (VUL 23:5; NRSV 24:5), that's to say, from the Lord Jesus, his savior.

The sooner he cries out to him for help, the sooner he'll hear you from high heaven, no matter where you are or what the danger.

Remember when the disciples were navigating the stormy sea? They thought they were going to drown and shouted out for Jesus by name. And what do you know? He came at once. Two of the evangelists recorded the story and what Jesus said. "Why are you afraid? Have faith. I'm here. Don't be afraid" (Mark 4:40; Matthew 8:26).

There's nothing quite like hearing the voice of Jesus. It's sweet enough to bring consolation! Strong enough to offer protection! Happy enough to restore joy! Benign enough to offer comfort! Graceful enough to dole out eternal life! Amen.

∽∾∽∾∽∾∽∾∽

CORPUS CHRISTI AND EUCHARISTIC DEVOTION

In the present chapter Kempis refers to the Sacrament of the Altar at least twice.

"Happy is he who's called to the supper of the lamb; he welcomes the sacrament until he can arrive at the final convivium."

"When the faithful communicates devoutly, or the priest celebrates reverently, he may be said to have dined with Jesus and his blessed mother."

Perhaps some historical background is called for.

The feast of *Corpus Christi* (Body of Christ) was a relatively new one in Kempis's time. The church already commemorated the Last Supper on Maundy Thursday, but the remembrance, coming as it did in Holy Week, was overshadowed by the sadness of Christ's passion and death.

Perhaps it was only a matter of time before the faithful had a feast of the Eucharist that was one of pure joy, celebrating not so much the effects of Christ's passion and death as his real presence among us in the Sacrament of the Altar. Its chief manifestations are adoration of the Eucharist and eucharistic processions through the streets. It was adopted in Liège in 1247, Cologne in 1306, Worms in 1315, Strasburg in 1316, and England by 1325.

According to Huizinga, Europe's streets were already full of processions for "executions and other public acts of justice, hawking, marriages and funerals" (9–10), so why not the Eucharist?

Kempis's own piety in this regard came to full bloom in "The Sacrament of the Altar," the fourth part of his *Imitation of Christ.* He begins it with Jesus exhorting a devout.

"Here are some of my sayings on the subject of Holy Communion, as recorded by my evangelists.

"Come to me, all you who labor and lumber, and I'll take up your load," wrote Matthew (11:28).

"The bread I give you is Mm flesh — there's enough to nourish the world," wrote John (6:57).

"Take it and eat it — this is my body. Do it again, whenever you think of me; it's in remembrance of my part in the original deal." Matthew recorded that too (26:76), and so did Paul (1 Corinthians 11:26).

"The devout who communicates me in this way — that's to say, who commemorates me by eating my flesh and drinking my blood — he'll take up residence with me, and I with him!" John again (5:64).

"These words I've spoken to you — breathe them and live" John too (6:63). — W.G.

14

Battling against the Vices

Take a risk,
and your heart will know the difference.

(Psalm VUL 30:25; NRSV 31:24)

Through the passion and cross of Christ and the pangs of the holy martyrs, we've learned to put up with adversities.

Through the blessed virgin Mary and all the saintly virgins, widows, and married continents, we've learned to control the carnal vices, condemn the sins of wealth, flee medals and decorations, and through contempt of worldly things seek heavenly things and prefer them to all others.

Servant of God, do strive to follow the patience of these brave people. Resist the devil and his advice. Reject and spurn all the entertainments of the flesh along with all the other vices. As a model use the virginal constancy of poor defenseless girls [like St. Agnes].

If God gave you temporal goods as a sign of his clemency toward your poverty, don't refuse them. Say yes, and be grateful about it. Don't be a dunce! But don't let your heart get attached! Why? Because you don't know how long you're going to be here or how much you'll be able to enjoy them.

Don't yearn for a long life, but do lust for a good life. Why? Because a good conscience is better than all the treasures of the world.

The more you have of earthly things, the lengthier your final reckoning will be.

The grace of the world is false, and the glory of the world brief, if the rich and famous prelates and their luxurious lifestyle are any indication. After them the deluge, that's to say, pains and tears and the devil breathing fire. There's no redemption from punishments like that.

What a joy it is when the elect move into the same neighborhood as the angels! It's where the greatest collection of felicities is located.

How happy the men! How prudent the virgins! They left all for Christ, and the road they traveled was narrow and not without difficulties. But they finally arrived at their eternal home.

Therefore, all faithful and devoted servants of Jesus Christ, know that you have to fight, watch, pray, fast, and labor as long as you live against an enormous menu of carnal and spiritual temptations.

You have to keep the flesh down with a whip. If you don't, it will rise up against you and make demands the spirit wouldn't approve of. That will help prevent your soul from being dragged against its will to gehenna.

What does it profit the flesh to eat elaborately prepared meals when afterward it will have to undergo a hellish indigestion?

And what advantage do you get by being praised and honored by the movers and shakers? In the future you'll only be confounded and condemned along with the impious and the devilish.

In the university world a professor has a reputation; among the elect he's just another bloke. But if he makes a fuss in the presence of God and the saints, he's going to receive nothing but bad evaluations.

To suffer for Christ and be thought of as just another bloke by the malevolent, that's the sort of thing that gets a standing ovation from God and all his saints.

To that end Jesus had some words for his disciples.

"Yes, there'll be consolation for all those faithful who suffered injury and stress because you're one of mine. Yes, you'll be rewarded in heaven, and you'd be surprised by how much, when they hate you and reproach you in public because you belong to me."

For the previous remarks I have Matthew's gospel to thank (5:11–12).

Amen.

∽∾∽∾∽∾∽∾

FLAGELLATION

Earlier in *Lilies,* in chapters 2, 3, and 14, Kempis recommended flagellation as a spiritual practice. "A few strokes inflicted upon one's own shoulders from to time has a remedial, humbling effect" (3).

As novice master and spiritual director for decades, he urged upon his charges, whether male or female, the discipline; indeed it was the discipline of the *disciplina,* the Latin word that came to mean the whip, scourge, discipline. Scripture references abound.

In the Old Testament first mention of the whip appears in Exodus. "Pharaoh's overseers scourged the ones supervising the Israelites with whips and words. 'Why is today's quota of bricks less than yesterday's'?" (5:14, 16). In 2 Paralipomenon (3 Kings) Roboam said, "My father beat you with whips, but I'll beat you with scorpions," that's to say, with whips into which pieces of metal had been embedded (12:11, 14).

In the New Testament, Jesus laid the whip on the money-changers (John 2:15). Five times Paul received the customary Roman punishment (thirty-nine stripes or lashes); three time he was beaten with rods (2 Corinthians 11:24, 25).

No wonder scourging found its way into monastic rules and councils, first to preserve community discipline — for serious offenses, young monks were scourged — and as a means of private penance and mortification.

In the eleventh century Peter Damien (1007–72), monk, bishop, cardinal, wrote a treatise on self-flagellation, and his praise prompted its practice in respectable convents and monasteries. But large-scale abuse was sure to follow. In the thirteenth century the Flagellants appeared, brotherhoods and sisterhoods who managed to turn public self-flagellation into edifying if bloodthirsty entertainment; of course, they were urging repentance and reformation.

Flashing forward to the twenty-first century, the urge to do more for the Lord in a physical way is as strong as it's ever been. The bloody realism of the Gibson film, *The Passion of the Christ,* not only showed Jesus being scourged but aroused in viewers the urge to share in the pain, if only in a paltry personal way.

Hence, since it's impossible to dissuade holy people from trying to please the Lord even in this most extravagant manner, here are a few guidelines.

First, never enter upon a program of self-flagellation without first getting permission from a spiritual director and then reporting back to that person. Happily, rare is the spiritual director who'd allow the practice.

Second, if one breaks the skin or raises a welt, or if, God forbid, blood is drawn, then one has gone too far. Discomfit should be the physical goal, not disfigurement.

All of which is another way of saying, if and when the urge to do something physical for the Lord arises, do one of three things.

Good, recognize that building one's spiritual life on mechanical practices — I would add to the discipline such items as the hair shirt and the chain, a wiry prickly device worn around arms or legs for limited periods of time — is folly.

Better, read chapter 12 of *Lilies* in which Kempis himself points out alternatives to corporal austerity.

Best, do something helpful or kind to the neighbor next door who's annoying you to death. Now that's a good practice, a spiritually healthy exercise, and one that Kempis advises in all of his writings.

Remember, the motive is one of remembrance, one of mortification; it's not payback to Jesus for what he suffered for us. Alas, for this we're in debt forever. — W.G.

15

Keeping a Steady Hand

When it comes to the work of the Lord,
no pranks, no stunts;
just keep a steady hand.

(1 Corinthians 15:58)

Tell me something, good brother. You have the ability to see and to hear. So how come you have trouble getting to the kingdom of heaven?

Blessed is the bloke who has sense enough to guard his heart and soul from wandering off; he's just the fellow who when he does return from a toot, confesses and receives forgiveness.

Shame on you, wandering off whenever you feel like it! It's such a waste of time for yourself and such a scandal to others.

The one who remains at home in his room achieves great peace — hanging out alone with Jesus, often talking in prayer with him, reading the Bible, studying each book methodically, dwelling affectively upon this passage and that.

Sadly the person with time on his hands often fills it by reading novels and other nonsensical tales; from the devil's point of view, he's ripe for the plucking. Such reading also separates him from the conversation of the community, where help of all sorts is only an arm's length away. My fear is that it'll infect the meek and the mild; it may even scandalize them with examples of unholy language and unmistakable gestures.

Yes, I'm talking to you, you the dissolute and whimsical. You're the ones who should fear the future torments of the fire of purgatory. From the devil's steel-tipped whips, you'll receive a stripe for each careless word and malignant thought.

Isn't it much better to fear now and thus to avoid the necessity of doing penance and making tears later? The other side of purgatory is hell, where one is housed with outrageous company and tortured without end.

One sure thing is that there's no joking or horsing around in the flames of hell; no such relief can be brought to bear.

If a person takes hell seriously, and there's no reason why he shouldn't, he'll quickly change his mind about the wonderfulness of all mundane things and begin to abhor all the entertainments of the flesh. All these have to do with after-death experiences, that's to say, avoiding eternal punishments and greeting celestial joys.

And there's more trouble, especially for those who pay decent enough attention to the divine judgments but somehow think that they're aimed at the simpleminded. How could they think that? Because they've never experienced these punishments firsthand.

16

Consoling
the Down-and-Out

*In the world you face pressure, you feel stress.
But be of good cheer. I've got the world in my pocket.*
(John 16:33)

There's a proverb favored by many. *The only comfort for the
wretched is a companion just as wretched.* Which is no consolation for the rest of us. But who does know how to pal around
with the down and out?

Well, there's one. His credentials may be found in the gospels. He appeared as a doctor and pastor of souls and consoler
of the down and out; as for us, he suffered and died on the
cross. On more than one occasion he made the following ob-
servation. "The healthy don't need the doctor; it's the sickly
who need round-the-clock care" (Matthew 9:12; Mark 2:17;
Luke 5:31). Yes, it's our Lord Jesus Christ.

On the same theme the holy David had this to say. "God's
at the side of those whose hearts are sore" (VUL 33:19;
NRSV 34:18).

And again, in another psalm. "When there's a temptation brewing, I'm at your side; I know how to get you out

of it; I know how to restore your reputation" (VUL 90:15; NRSV 91:15).

Depression has many varietals, but the balm that works best is this. Christ was tempted, saddened, and pained many times for us.

Look at it another way. It if weren't practical and indeed helpful for our souls to sweat it out in this world, God wouldn't permit it. After all he has this reputation of being good and just. But that didn't mean he'd spare his son from the whip. So who are you to say, "Sorry, I don't do whips" — you who've committed so many sins in your short life?

It's not right for an officious yet suspicious servant to tell his master that he's doing it all wrong. After all, the servant has felt only a few twinges of pain in his lifetime, but God's own son, who loved sinners but had committed no sins himself, was whipped senseless for us.

It's only right then for the spiritually sick who want to leave their sickness behind to drink from the same cup as Jesus; there is no need to gulp it down; a sip or two will do. After all, any doctor worth his salt would down a bitter draft if it would get rid of death, heal the bedridden, and free him from eternal death. Just the thought of the great load the innocent Lord labored under would alleviate the pathetic load the guilty servant felt. Indeed, it's a form of pain management. If the long-term patient thought for one second that bearing his affliction with a smile correlated with his purgation of sins, with the hope of eternal salvation thrown in, then he'd grin from ear to ear.

What a great honor it would be if the poor servant donned the clothes Jesus wore and draped his own shoulders with the purple cloak thrown over the Lord's.

Jesus's consistent dress was humility of heart and poverty of pocket, patience in adversity and perseverance in virtue.

Welcoming the lash of the Lord as a gift will find salvation of soul coming with each stripe; and he'll receive quite a nice crown in heaven.

The psalmist put it this way. "Happy the one who comes to know the down and out" (VUL 40:2; NRSV 41:1); Jesus did that, and did it without clothes or resources. The human being who did that would find himself the richest person in the universe.

Who's the person we should follow? The one who patiently bears his cross for the rest of his life, at which happy time he'll find that his soul has made the final cut.

17

Putting Conscience on a Leash

I hold my soul in my hands.

(Psalm VUL 118:109; NRSV 119:109)

For the soul who's devoted to this life, there's nothing better to think about than the search for eternal life.

He should read everything he can get his hands on; he should review all the arguments. The proposition? *There's no salvation for the soul except in God and the godly life.*

Along these lines the Lord and Redeemer of Souls made many remarks to his disciples; this was how Matthew remembered it. "What does it profit a person if he gains the whole world but loses his own soul?" (16:28).

A person shouldn't think of his soul's salvation as just another amusing trinket; actually, it's the eternal prize. The person who thinks wisely in this regard is truly a wise negotiator, preferring the eternal and spiritual to the stuff with an expiration date.

Who's a good and faithful servant of Christ's? The person with two talents who worked them into four? The one with five talents who doubled his stake? The one who, instead of hiding it or burying it or tossing it or spurning it, gave it to a poor person so that he could pray for himself?

I think the answer is obvious. That's to say, offering a tiddle in thanks to the Lord would seem a modest gift, but God welcomes it as though it was a spectacular one.

Happy the servant who's reliable; no stranger to the market, he makes the best use of the temporal goods he works with on a daily basis. About the rest of the stuff that has nothing to do with this world, the servant doesn't have a great deal to say. Seeing only what God wants him to see and hearing only what God wants him to hear, he passes through the rough waters of life with an even keel. Yes, he carries his soul in his hand, lest it fall and break.

The moral?

Don't get curious about the status of others, spiritual or otherwise, except when the charity of God or fraternal compassion demands it.

Don't seek the praises of humankind, not a hallowed word among them, hollow words all! Don't dread the vituperations that come your way unless, of course, they should apply; turn them to your own advantage; let them purge your soul, deregulate your high self-esteem, and, eventually, afford a rather nice crown in high heaven.

No one has a right to expect help from God above except, perhaps, the person who's inserted himself into the fray between God and the devil.

A prayer.

You suffered for me, Lord God, so I should suffer for you and as much as I can. As you once said to Saint Peter, which was overheard by John. "Follow me" (21:19).

Alas, O Lord, I've suffered for you, yes, but far too little.

I often propose to do ten things; if I'm lucky, I finish one. My words are many; my works, few. The whole thing is my fault, and I have no real excuse. The sloth and negligence are mine own, and my sins increase. So what good does it do me to think and say these things except to seek and pray for forgiveness?

I have sinned, O Lord; have mercy on me. All the saints in your heavenly court have done so before me, and they learned their lessons; and all the faithful alive today are doing this very thing.

All saints and friends of God, pray for me. I'm weak, I've no resources left, and so I humbly pray for your help.

Praying Like a Pauper

Holy God of mine, Lord of all the saints. Bend your ear to hear my prayer. Help me, keep me afloat, until I learn to navigate (Psalm VUL 118:117; NRSV 119:117).

Would that I deserved to be one of your prancing flock, the one you prepared in your heavenly kingdom for your humble admirers.

I should love you, Lord, Lord of my virtue, love of my heart. That's what your commandment ordered me to do. You're my hope, my salvation, my total desire.

Sweep the dust kittens out of my intellect — I need the clarity when I confront the error.

Deterge the grunge in my heart — a clean soul is the only way to confront impurity.

Stiffen my faith — doubt makes me kind of wobbly.

Firm up my hope — diffidence solves things by pillow fights.

Heat up my charity — there's nothing worse than week-old bread.

Spin out my patience — every rumpus and ruckus has to be covered.

Connect my prayer — the devil tries to disconnect it.

Focus my attention when it comes to reading — reading sometimes scatters the mind.

Keep me busy — anything as an antidote against tedium or just plain dozing off.

Call to mind your sacred passion — I get antsy about the vices prickling my soul.

Stick around when I attempt all these, O Lord — whisper me words of encouragement. Amen.

SILENCE AND SOUND

In the present chapter, "Putting Conscience on a Leash," and in the next chapter, "Keeping One's Distance," Kempis mentions another facet of medieval life, silence and sound. Here's what Huizinga had to say about it.

The contrast between silence and sound, darkness and light, like that between summer and winter, was more strongly marked than it is in our lives. The modern town hardly knows silence or darkness in their purity, nor the effect of a solitary light or a single distant cry.

All things presenting themselves to the mind in violent contrasts and impressive forms lent a tone of excitement and of passion to everyday life and tended to produce that perpetual oscillation between despair and distracted joy, between cruelty and pious tenderness which characterize life in the Middle Ages.

One sound rose ceaselessly above the noises of busy life and lifted all things unto a sphere of order and serenity, the sound of bells. The bells were in daily life like good spirits which, by their familiar voices, now called upon the citizens to mourn and now to rejoice, now warned them of danger, now exhorted them to piety. They were known by their names: big Jacqueline, or the bell Roland. Everyone knew the difference in meaning of the various ways of ringing. However continuous the ringing of the bells, people would seem not to have become blunted to the effect of their sound....

What intoxication the pealing of all the bells of all the churches and of all the monasteries of Paris must have produced, sounding from morning till evening, and even during the night, when a peace was concluded or a pope elected! (10–11). —W.G.

18

Keeping One's Distance

Yes, I've put in a long distance between me and thee,
and yet I remain where I was, alone and with you.
No wonder I'm afraid.

(Psalm VUL 54:8; NRSV 55:7)

Sometimes it's a good thing to lie low, hide out, especially if you want peace of heart or a place to pray. Having a secret place, a getaway spot, often helps. The principle? A fish out of water isn't long for this world; and a monk outside his cloister is easily distracted and prone to mischief.

A buzzing bee collecting honey wastes no time returning to its secret spot for the deposit; if he didn't, there'd be no food for the winter. It even smothers the sweet smell lest the other insects steal it in midflight.

Now aromas are precious things. Shut up in a pyxis, the aromas are heavy, strong; once the flowers open and the petals are on show, their perfumes linger, then float away.

There is another point here. Flowers once touched by human hands begin to decline; that's to say, the human touch begins to encroach on the septa of fruit within, and their high walls begin to buckle.

Roses in a garden increase in size when the buds are securely closed. But when the petals dry, they fall and are stepped on.

So the monk who makes a habit of being outside the monastery loses his charism; he's just another itinerant, unstable bloke in religious garb wandering the streets. If only he'd stayed inside, he'd have a shot at being regarded as a saint.

A burning candle is quickly extinguished by a breeze; put it in a lamp, and it'll burn forever. So the fervor of devotion, which can be so easily snuffed in a breezeway, burns brightly in the privacy of one's own room.

What can I say? Love one's room and the silence it provides. If you want to be devout and peaceful, then stay inside.

You have to be strong, always on guard. Why? Because you can't go outside and do minor damage in dealing with externs without at the same time suffering major damage to your soul.

It's your choice, but if you value your spiritual life, then learn to enjoy the solitude of your digs. The blessed virgin Mary spent a lot of quiet time in her space; God took advantage of this devotion, sending a heavenly angel to talk to her.

May your angel, your guardian angel, chat you up with heavenly news and keep you toeing the mark. And may you leave the dark angel with his wallet full of dirty pictures far behind you.

One devout lover of silence summed up his own experience. *I rarely speak with others and then not for long, but still I feel my conscience has been compromised in some way.* Certainly a sentiment worth noting.

A second put it this way. *Silence has the power to change things for the better.* A foundational thought if there ever was one!

A third one had this take. *If you're going to say something, wait for the right time to say it.* A noble thought!

A fourth offered this. *Learn to keep your mouth shut. That way you don't tell stories about others, and you won't lie.*

Summing up. *The wonderful thing about silence is that it prevents you from talking trash.*

Many people say many things; hence, slips of the tongue are inevitable.

Praise the person who makes silence his special virtue.

Upbraid the blabbermouth.

When you do speak, avoid double meanings, flee the rowdy crowd, love the secret place, follow the humble and devout person, put up with irritation — all for Christ who was crucified for you.

A junior brother asked this question of a senior brother. *What's in our foundational documents about peace and devotion?*

And this was the senior's response. *There are three rules. Labor instead of leisure. Reading instead of resting (reading is a fine antidote to tedium). God instead of Satan. These three the holy fathers of old have praised.*

The brother who's silent divines the sacred mysteries more easily.

The monk who's got the latest book in his pocket and makes the rounds of the city for the latest news has done nothing to deserve the heavenly gifts; and worse, his bad behavior is contagious to others.

The proud person has trouble zipping his lips.

The educated person wants to be seen and heard and praised over others.

The presumptuous person is an object of ridicule by others.

The truly silent person merits grace from bystanders.

It takes great humility of heart to think less than complimentary things about oneself and at the same time only complimentary things about others who aren't half as good as oneself.

Pride runs riot in the senses, and stands contrary to the will of God. This leprosy is at its worst when it hates God; it may even lead to sudden death.

Humble obedience is always simple and innocent, everywhere joyful and secure.

A person of few words is a person worth a few remarks. Avoid light-headed ripostes; speak practical things.

Add a modicum of modesty to everything, and the life of virtue becomes more than attractive.

This is what Jesus had to say about it, at least as Mark recorded it. "Salt is good, a good seasoning. You should be seasoned too, well seasoned, and peace will surround you" (9:48–49).

Paul the apostle in his epistle to the Colossians, said much the same thing. "Everything you say should be seasoned with salt; that's to say, should have an edge to it" (4:6).

And holy Job. "How can one stomach something that hasn't been seasoned with salt?" (Job 6:6).

The chaste and modest person guards his heart, his mouth, and all his senses. Why? Because they're prone to sin against both God and neighbor.

The person who has no compunction in his heart has no compunction about hearing the latest news and spreading it about.

The person who doesn't keep close watch on his heart and mouth quickly kills off what grace of compunction he may have.

The monk isn't exempt from liking to talk; he easily exceeds his limit of words per day.

If you have Jesus crucified firmly fixed in your heart, a flashy or casual word wouldn't find it so easy to escape your mouth. But because you don't have him firmly fixed in your heart, you continue to look for frivolous entertainment outside the monastery, which is totally pathetic! All of which contributes little to alleviating the pains pressing on your heart.

Only Jesus is the true solace of your heart; only he can heal all the after-effects of vice.

It takes only a moment, it takes only a word, to free the soul from sin and its suffering.

Grace has more good than sin has evil.

Why do you listen to the news of the world? It only ruffles your mind and distracts your heart.

Why wouldn't you listen to the sermons of Christ? Now they're something that can restore the consolation to you.

A SEASONING FOR ALL SEASONS

In the present selection Kempis flavored his argument with several salient quotations from both testaments.

For Old and New Testament peoples, salt was a seasoning for all seasons. It came from rock formations and from salt water that had evaporated. With the Dead Sea nearby, Israelites had more salt than they could use.

According to Ezekiel, newborns were washed with a saline solution (16:24). According to Leviticus (2:13) and Ezekiel (42:24), salt connoted purity and so was used in sacrificial offerings. In 2 Kings (2:19–22) Elisha purified a poisoned spring with salt. In Numbers (18:18) and 2 Chronicles (13:5) a covenant of salt had the force of an oath of fidelity. In Judges (9:45) and Deuteronomy (29:23) salt was the invader's final insult, spreading it around to kill future growth.

In New Testament times Jesus said to his disciples, "You're the salt of the earth, but beware, even salt can lose its taste." His remarks were picked up by Matthew (5:13), Mark (9:48–49), and Luke (14:34). Jesus had to be referring to rock salt, crushed and then broadcast over prepared soil as a fertilizer.

In *Mottos for Monks,* Kempis wrote, "No table is fully set if the bread or salt is missing. And no fare is nourishing if the Scriptures aren't read aloud. If it isn't the Holy Scriptures, then it's just a barrage of verbiage" (4). Here he seemed to indicate that bread was the Scripture and salt was the reading aloud.

—W.G.

19

Possessing Nothing

The pauper stares at you;
the orphan won't let go of your sleeve.

(Psalm VUL 9:35 / {10:14}; NRSV 10:14)

Compulsory poverty has its bright spots. God helps in hard times, consoles in tough times. He's the one and only hope *in extremis,* the crown of glory in the kingdom of eternal beatitude.

Voluntary poverty assumed for Christ isn't far behind. What a precious virtue it is, and worthy of eternal reward with the angels in heaven; no thief is a-thieving there, no looter a-looting or killer a-killing either.

Amid the many dangers of daily life, the riches of this age may be found, but free is the servant of Christ who renounces everything that belongs to this world.

Odd thing! Possessing nothing, the pauper and the pooper possess everything in Christ.

Hanging naked on the cross, he didn't have a spot to rest his head on; he couldn't move his hands or his feet. Who can match the master's poverty in such an unglamourous moment as this? No one else. "Because his name is exalted, blessed, over all the things of heaven and earth" (Psalm 148:13).

O good poverty! If God hadn't been poor, you'd be ungrateful for all the miseries laid upon you.

The spirit of poverty has done its job when the eyes like nothing they see. The principle? See no evil — do no evil.

He's truly poor in spirit when he doesn't lord his good words or deeds over others, and doesn't seek a higher status than he already has.

Poverty of soul opens the gate of heaven, increases the crown of glory, and wins the martyrs' palm of patience. This is what it truly means to serve Christ faithfully.

Blessed the person who makes virtue out of his own necessity and infirmity, no matter what drudge follows the will of God.

Therefore, dear pauper, don't let your gloom get the better of you when your pockets are empty; and don't get huffy when people insult you, or friends leave you behind.

Convert your heart to Christ, who became in debt and infirm for you; seek your solace from God and God alone, that's to say, if you really want the joy as much as you say you do.

All consolations sought outside the monastery are no consolations at all. They're flipflops; that's to say, they seem to do the trick at the time, but they don't really satisfy for long.

So, as your special friend and relative choose Jesus Christ son of God; as for the rest of your scruffy friends, lose them.

Avoid teaming up with a person who wants to get in the way of your holy service of Christ, and that other person who wants to drag you through the terrors of the age down to the portals of hell.

"The highway to hell has many lanes, and many there are who hurtle down it," said the Lord; the evangelist Matthew recorded it (7:13).

The Lord is more solace than any one human, or all humans combined, can handle. What's more, he can give visas for the next world to all incoming immigrants.

"This world has its moments," wrote John in his first letter (2:17); smoke curling upward, flowers budding firmly, and then the wind leaving wisps and petals behind.

Therefore, brother, poor though you may be, stay the course in the service of God. Remain with your brothers in the many tasks that keep this monastery going; remember, you chose to put God first. Yes, leave behind your parents and relatives, and do it of your own free will, not because we ask you to do it; offer yourself wholly to God that you may enjoy the kingdom of Christ in heaven with all the angels.

Such a deal! A little labor, a little dolor, and in return eternal rest in heaven.

Take another look, a long look this time, at the wounds of Christ and the ugly ulcers of the poor Lazarus. Such a sight will ease the agony as you prepare to die and pass from this world.

RICH MAN, POOR MAN

In the present chapter, "Possessing Nothing," and the following chapter, "Possessing Everything," Kempis makes mention of the parable of a rich man, Dives the millionaire, and a poor man,

Lazarus the leper. Here is a paraphrasal rendering of that parable as found in the gospel of Luke (16:19–31).

Why a parable? Because it was Jesus' best way of communicating with the uneducated and unsophisticated. Alas, it was also the best way to communicate with the Pharisees who, despite their education and sophistication, often missed the simplest point. And perhaps it's not the worst way to communicate with the modern world.

Once upon time there was a man who was rich. His name was Dives. He wore royal purple overalls and white Egyptian underalls. And he ate like a king.

At the door to his residence, there lay a poor leper named Lazarus. His skin was covered with running sores. He hadn't eaten in days. All he wanted to do, he kept telling the person at the door, was to recover for himself the scraps and crumbs that fell from the rich man's table. The butler would let him in reluctantly, but the dogs were friendly enough; they came and licked his wounds.

To make a long story short, both men died. Lazarus was carried by angels into the presence of Abraham. Dives was plunged into deepest hell. In his torments he'd raise his eyes and see in the distance Abraham at the messianic banquet dining with his new friend, Lazarus.

"Father Abraham," cried Dives, "have mercy on me. I know that guy. He's a bum. Used to hang around my place. Send him down. All I want him to do is dip his finger into some water and let the drops fall on my tongue. Why? Because, to tell you the truth, I'm burning up!"

"Son," replied Abraham from afar. "Remember all the good times you had in life? Well, all Lazarus had in his life was bad times. Now it's his turn to enjoy and your time to suffer. Besides, between you and us there's a great chasm; we can't go to you, and you can't come to us."

"Okay," said Dives, "if you won't do me that, would you do me this? Send the bum to my father's house. My five brothers still live there. He could tell them about this place of torment and warn them that if they don't change their ways, they're coming here too."

"Already they have Moses!" shouted Abraham. "Already they have the prophets! What else do they need to know about Torment House?"

"But the lads won't listen to the old geezers," cried Dives. "Someone from here should rise from the dead and go to them and tell them the real story, then they'll listen to him."

"Well," said Abraham, "if the lads have no ear for Moses and the prophets, then they certainly won't listen to a dead man who just happens to drop by."

Luke didn't record whether this story with its several applications about money and the law made a dent in the Pharisees. But it's still a good story and indeed a well-traveled one. According to the *Harper Bible Commentary,* "versions of it are found in rabbinic as well as Egyptian literature" (1034b).

As for Kempis himself, he had personal experience of being an almoner for his monastery, dispensing spiritual as well as material charity at the monastery gate. Like everything else related to the monastery, he wrote it up. The result, a short but classic treatise entitled "Posting for the Food and Wine Cellar," or, as it is commonly called, "The Faithful Steward."

Here is what Kempis had to say about the job. "When presented with two candidates for the office of steward," he wrote, "pick the one who has more faith and prudence, and then turn him loose on the business" (1).

Bread was always in long supply in the monastery, but even during lean times Kempis would take the last loaf the monks had and cut it in half for the one who'd just rung the bell at the gate. And he offered spiritual help as well. To a leper not unlike Lazarus, he said the following.

"Even though your skin is a running sore and your stomach a clenched fist, rejoice in the Lord. For the scraps denied to you now, you'll have a splendid spread in the Father's hall and the bread of heaven at the Son's table. Instead of dogs licking your wounds, you'll have angels binding them with balm."

These and other such remarks may be found in Kempis's "Consolations for the Down and Out." As preface to this short work, he set down his rationale. "As the Lord God said to his people in despair, so I say to you down-and-outs today. *I will be your Consolation — Consolation is my middle name*" (Isaiah 40:1). — W.G.

20

Possessing Everything

I'm penniless, and I'm in pain; help me, God!

(Psalm VUL 69:6; NRSV 70:5)

This is the voice of the sick poor, gasping for God and his kingdom.

If you yourself are poor and infirm, hang in there. You're in pain, yes, but only for a short time. What does it matter that you have no money for food or clothes? Life is short, and so is the pain.

In the meantime you should thank God. Such a gift! Yes, I know you're being eaten alive by the symptoms of the down-and-out now. But better now than later when you'll be crucified in the inferno with the rich and famous.

Recall your past sins? They've often offended God and neighbor; bear the rod of the Lord as remission for your sins. No, you haven't satisfied the temporal punishment due to them.

If it's any consolation to you, remember the troubles of the saints and the wounds of Christ. He was cut to ribbons and yet bore up under the lash for you.

If it's any comfort to you, remember Lazarus, that poor, flea-bitten, ulcerous heap under the rich man's table. As Luke recalled it, after his death he was welcomed into Abraham's bosom. Something else to remember. Dives came to a sad end, as do many of the rich and famous. When he died, he was buried in hell, a prison from which there's no return.

These two courses are presented to you. Either suffer now like the dyspeptic Lazarus and rejoice ever after with Christ. Or live the lovely life of a healthy rich man, only to die suddenly and burn with the devil. Pick one.

A few words are all an intelligent person needs before making a decision. Understanding the evils in his life and removing them in a timely fashion will make him a happy man. Yes, the motive here is fear of being damned with the impious, crucified with whippings.

No words are enough for the not-so-intelligent when making a decision like this. Warnings from the holy books are in one ear and out the other; they initiate no corrections. Alas, his fate is sealed: scourgings, whippings, countless lacerations, with no end in sight.

On the other hand there's Lazarus, preeminent among the sick poor! He's a free man, borne by angels to Abraham's bosom. Just look back at the favors God showered on him. No rich friends coming to visit him, no servants or companions serving his needs, only dogs coming to lick his weeping wounds.

From the mouth of Lazarus came not a murmur of complaint, just thanks and praise. Human piety denied him solace, but a pack of dogs did him some kindness.

Yes, you too are infirm in a spiritual way. Don't complain if you're left unconsoled and don't be agitated by your infirmities, real or imagined. Just think to yourself that something good will come out of divine mercy, and that you won't die having been cut to bits or burnt to a crisp.

Lazarus was perhaps a small and sometime sinner, but you're a grave and frequent sinner.

Therefore, bear with patience the dolors of the infirm, and pay no mind to those who consider you a derelict. In the end, as with Lazarus, you'll deserve to enter the gate of heaven.

21

Understanding
Sacred Scripture

Reveal your words, unveil your meanings;
everyone has a right to know, even the children.

(Psalm VUL 118:130; NRSV 119:130)

A number of things have been written in the Old and New Testaments having to do with the doctrine of the soul. Their purpose is simple: to help us serve God faithfully by hating sin and clinging to God with a good heart — that's to say, a pure heart — now and in the future.

If you don't know anything about these matters, humbly seek out someone who does. If your knowledge of them is a bit short, hie yourself to the nearest professor.

As the psalmist has sung, "Reveal your words, unveil your meanings; the children want to know."

If you can't grasp the complexities of scripture scholarship, then at least come to grips with its simplicities. Jesus himself gave us the clue. Whenever he and his friends made a stop, children came a-running. "Don't shoo them off!" he shouted, at least as Matthew recorded it. "I've got the time. Let them come in. After all, heaven is a lot like a playground" (19:14).

Scripture studies do have their complexities, but if they drive you crazy, don't break your head over it. Just commit them to the Holy Spirit and believe the Scriptures are true. Why? Because the Holy Spirit is the doctor, the professor, of all truth; he can't be party to falsity.

Many people have doubts, all kinds of them, but the fault or defect isn't necessarily in the Scriptures. It's just that we have a blind spot or that we've only dipped into the Holy Books and not read enough in them. In net they contain all the information we need for eternal salvation.

All that being said, read these Scriptures, the canonical Scriptures, till your eyes fall out. Break only for prayer and Mass.

Odd thing, during prayer and Mass scriptural knots tend to unravel. But this doesn't happen to just anybody, only to devouts. Knots remain knots for scholars whose only interest in the Scriptures is intellectual complexity.

Funny thing, the Holy Books are actually aimed at children and other unschooled folk with simple vocabularies; the subtleties, however, can cause some major damage. Hence it helps if obscure words, phrases, and sayings are explained.

The monks who pay attention to the readings in choir or refectory are usually the ones who can handle the historical and biblical vocabularies. For them every word of God they hear or read is a drop of honey.

The longer a reader lives, the more the Scriptures reveal to him. At death day he still won't be angelic, but after he's breathed his last he'll become beatific; that's to say, arrival in heaven will surely clear all things up.

Solid, hearty food isn't quite right for the very young or seriously sick. Soft foods and brothy liquids are best for them.

Simple organs and modest chants make sound and give joy; beer-garden ballads, on the other hand, are like rolling thunder; far from offering some recreation to the infirm, they scare the living daylights out of them.

Sudden lightning blinds the eyes; eternal light, on the other hand, actually sharpens one's vision.

Dangerous undercurrents drag dumb swimmers under; for them bridges across bodies of water would make more sense.

Often on a journey it's not uncommon to see a lamb gamboling about the same plot on which a cow is being slaughtered.

If one has simple belief and humble obedience, he'll find grace, but if he relies on his own resources, he'll lose what little he has.

High concepts tend to titillate the proud, but in the end they confound those who glory in their knowledge.

I've seen the simple weep out of devotion during prayer. Noisemakers when they pray make a lot of fuss, but they don't have a prayerful sentiment in their heart.

How does this happen? Because the simple and humble strive to please God in everything they do and say. The rollicking voice of the simple heart may be heard skipping about in God's heavenly house; the wistful voice of the wandering heart lingers in the byways and bywaters of a city-state.

Pay serious attention to the psalms. Don't rush through them as if you're trying to win a race; read and sing them slowly, quietly. The result? A great sweetness will descend upon your devotion.

Yes, the Lord looks kindly on the right of heart, that's to say, to those who seek his glory, not their own.

Blessed are the words that come tumbling from the mouth of a speaker or singer, especially when they turn the soul of the listener to compunction.

Before the cock crows, he shakes the sleepers out of his wings, primes himself, gets himself pumped. Before correcting another, a monk should do the same, that's to say, correct himself.

When it comes time to teach, make the necessary preparation. Correct yourself before you urge another to make the same correction. In fact, the correction needed in another is really a mirror image of the correction you should be making in yourself.

The apostle Paul has given us a good example in this regard. I've put it into the form of prayerful conversation between him and me with me speaking first.

"Before you preached to others, you humbly admitted your own sins. 'Jesus Christ came into the world to free up sinners, and put me first among them,' you wrote in your first to Timothy. 'I'm not worthy to be called an apostle'" (1:15).

"Yes, I did."

"And why should that be, holy Paul?"

"Because I persecuted the church of God" (1 Corinthians 15:9).

"How come you're such a saint and venerable creature today?"

"It's got nothing to do with me or with anyone else. But it has everything to do with Jesus Christ. I learned from him how to be meek and mild and how to obey his gospel. Whatever I've done, and I've taught this, I ascribe principally to God. He called me through his grace to faith, which I now preach and serve until I die. 'By the grace of God I have become what I am' (15:10). I've never been lacking in grace; it remains in me and will always be there until I arrive at the house of the one who redeemed and saved me with his blood."

22

Talking Straight

In your patience you'll possess your souls.

(Luke 21:19)

When someone speaks harshly to you or somebody blindsides you, don't fire right back. Instead, if you must open your mouth, speak humbly, and keep your cool as Jesus would do in the same situation.

Remember that passage in Matthew? "He was accused by the crowd, and not a peep came from him; he was whipped by the soldiers, and not even a murmur" (26:63).

If the need arises and something may be accomplished by speaking, then respond nicely and make your point prudently. That's how Christ, made a punching bag by the soldiers and quizzed by the servant of the high priest, responded, that's to say, with straight talk, not double-talk. John has retold the story (22:23).

If you want to free yourself from confusion, you have to build other people up.

Keep your patience no matter what the contradictions or objections. Just pay attention to the progress of your own soul. Here the virtue of patience will stand you in good stead. It plants the soul with virtues and leads to the palm of martyrdom.

Back to Jesus Christ and his passion.

According to Luke, when he was accused by the high priests and the elders of the people, he said nothing (23:9). That's to say, he did himself what he had advised others to do.

"Take it from me; I'm meek and humble of heart; do the same, and your souls will find the living easy" (Matthew 11:29).

You won't find it elsewhere, real rest and peace without fear, except in God alone, in true humility and benign patience; in an environment like that, adversity doesn't have a chance.

May God be your total hope.

Don't deposit your hope in any creature, large or small.

Without God all things are hollowed; with God, they're all hallowed.

∾∾∾∾∾∾∾∾

CLOTHES

The Brothers and Sisters of the Common Life and the Augustinian Monastery and Convent drew both men and women from all ranks of society. But the new dress code and the new spirituality would be harder on the rich candidates; this, according to Huizinga, is what they would have to give up.

No epoch ever witnessed such extravagance of fashion as that extending from 1350 to 1480. Here we can observe the unhampered expansion of the esthetic of the time. All the forms and dimensions of dress are ridiculously exaggerated.

The female head-dress assumes the conical shape of the hennin, *a form evolved from the little coif, keeping the hair under the kerchief. High and bombed foreheads are in fashion, with the temples shaved. Low-necked dresses made their appearance.*

The male dress had features still more bizarre — the immoderate length of the points of the shoes, called poulanines, *which the knights at Nicopolis had to cut off to enable them to flee; the laced waists, the balloon-shaped sleeves standing up at the shoulders; the too long* houppelandes *and the too short doublets; the cylindrical or pointed bonnets; the hoods draped about the head in the form of a cock's comb or flaming fire. A state costume was ornamented by hundreds of precious stones* (249–50).

Here's what Kempis had to say about clothes.

"Have you noticed that earthly joys enjoy only a half life? That's to say, that they don't last long? Right when you least expect it they expire, stain your clothes, offend your nose" (*Roses,* 5).

"It doesn't shrink from touching wounds, washing feet, making beds, laundering clothes, scrubbing stains" (*Roses,* 14).

"He who washes the hats and clothes of his brothers — it's like baptizing Jesus with John the Baptist" (*Roses,* 18).

"Look at Jesus on the cross, no clothes, nailed like a felon, and the pain of it all" (*Lilies,* 12).

"What a great honor it would be if the poor servant donned the clothes Jesus wore and draped his own shoulders with the purple cloak thrown over the Lord's. Jesus's consistent dress was humility of heart, poverty of pocket; patience in adversity, perseverance in virtue" (*Lilies*, 16).

"He came into the world with no clothes, and like a pauper and an exile he heads toward the tomb" (*Lilies*, 25). —W.G.

23

Fleeing Vices

Run, my beloved, run for your life!
(VUL Song of Songs 8:14; NRSV Song of Solomon 8:14)

What's to run from? Whenever people get together, bad things happen. That's why it's important to spend time alone with the Lord. Praying, studying, writing — good exercises all. They'll keep the vices at a distance. Yes, time well spent, and it sets a good example for others.

Take a walk outside the monastery, and you'll soon find yourself lapsing into double-talk. Rare it is that a soul returns unsullied and without distraction to his cell, where he's labored to cultivate peace.

Speak what's true, and you'll speak the truth. Speak with forked tongue, and you'll find yourself despised.

Don't go out looking for praise and approval.

The good you do belongs to God; the bad, to yourself.

Tell lies, and Christ will flee your heart. Tell the truth, and he'll return.

Put on airs, and you'll only hoodwink yourself.

Talk straight, and you'll be honored and admired.

We're all brothers created by one God, all sinners born of sinful parents, but through grace and baptism we are cleansed and united with Christ.

No one should condemn another. No one should deride another or cause pain in another. Instead he should be helpful to them, which is what he'd want for himself should he ever be in need.

Comfort those whose faith is infirm; use the holy words of Scripture. Fetch the bread of heaven for those caught in the toils.

Cheer up the sad; pour a draft for those who thirst for eternal life.

Choke the angry with chitchat. Pour honey on the tongue of detractors.

Bring silence to the scatter-brained; generate great peace among your brothers.

Prefer others to yourself; otherwise, you'll look like a blockhead to others and worthy of confusion.

Humble yourself in all things, and you'll earn more grace and glory.

Be pious and humble; pray, and you'll skirt the traps the devil has laid down for you. The poor proud person hasn't got a chance; he couldn't see a devilish trap to save his life, and so he perishes.

All of which is another way of saying, the pious Jesus guards us always and leads us to the joys of heaven.

24

Hurting the One You Want to Heal

Physician, heal thyself!
(Luke 4:23)

Always keep in mind, before you speak and ruffle somebody's feathers, that when you argue a point beyond a certain point or use any argument to make your point, your sin moves up from venial to mortal.

If you're just and prudent, you'll regulate the time and manner of speaking; that's to say, before you speak, you should take into account the person you're speaking to as well as the nature of humankind. The danger here is that you may hurt or harm the very one you want to heal.

The voice of the well-educated and very discreet is like a thick vessel adorned with gold and filled with oil, a soothing, healing substance with strong aroma.

Laypeople are edified by your good words and religious behavior. The lazy are aroused. The naysayers become convinced. The scatter-brained get their act together. The ignorant are instructed. The devout are inflamed.

Personal example is far more effective than speaking when it comes to convincing people to condemn the world and change their life. To accomplish just half, professors would have to speak volumes.

It's no big thing to teach others or to make others cringe, but to get a hold on oneself and to change one's own life for the better, this takes great wisdom, human as well as divine.

When in doubt, try to look on the bright side. Don't pass judgment on what you don't know. Avoid the obvious evils. Keep one's own scandalous behavior under wraps. Be supportive of the cricks and cranks of the sick. And what you can't do, commend to God's good care.

Keep in mind that God has been supportive of your many and varied activities to date, and that, even though you haven't done what you'd promised to do about your defects. Piously he tolerates you, waits for you. He expects you to learn more about your own infirmity and humbly seek forgiveness. Don't turn your back on anyone and don't jump to conclusions about anything.

Therefore, give your brother in Christ a free ride when it comes to his peccadillos. The same God has long given you freebies for your great indiscretions all along.

The devout and humble use only a few words; a barrage of verbiage has no place in the interior life.

The proud person speaks only in pronouncements. The irate person takes other people's heads off. The scrupulous person annoys the living daylights out of people who couldn't care less.

The meek and mild person puts up with the annoyances of the fearful; he prays more than he cringes; he condoles the sinner and proves himself a friend by his deeds.

When you put yourself ahead of others, you expose yourself to dangers and make yourself look like a chump.

The lover of vainglory can't keep his mouth shut for long; he thinks that the more he speaks, the more intelligent he sounds. He blushes when it comes to doing vile and servile tasks, or taking the last place in a line, or sitting at the far end of the hall.

Odd thing, the greatest honor is to show humility in all things, and to think of oneself as inferior to others, to serve Christ freely in all things. After all, he's the one who said, at least according to Luke, "Here I am sitting in the middle of you, and yet I'm the one who's waiting on you" (22:27).

When one is young, he has to learn when to be silent and when to speak. Otherwise the lad will leave his elders totally confused.

When it comes to speaking, it's safer to be silent than sorry.

It's a sign of wisdom to know when to be silent. It's also great wisdom to know when to speak modestly and what to say to those in the know.

The insipid don't know how to manage time or keep a semblance of order, that is why so many bad things happen to them; it serves them right. Youth is fearless and speaks fast; the same is true of the insipid.

If the know-it-alls listen and the scared-sillies hold their tongue, then hope will flower like a lily among the virtues.

Lady Pride stands for everything that God's against, and she can't acquiesce to the councils of senior women.

Yes, it's difficult to hold a tight rein on all of one's words and deeds, so some become religious for the solitude and silence and for the chance to engage in conversation with God.

25

Facing Uncertain Death

Keep watch because you don't know the day or the hour.

(Matthew 25:13)

Some happy thoughts.

Think often of your last hour. That's when everything in this life — the happy and sad, the honor and dishonor — closes down.

Think also of the poor little soul who made the journey for God. She spurned all the world had to offer, no matter how attractive they appeared to be.

In the last hour of the world the castles, villas, and towns will fall; the gold and silver vessels will crumble; the decorative metal trays will melt; the vases filled with aromatics will crack.

Also passing away will be lyres, horns, flutes; gaming, joking, pranking. No more standing ovations, songs, chants. Such great noises on the fields and in the houses! The living will quiver. The earth will quaver. Such a litany!

How wise it is now to think about all this. It will help you put the time between now and then into perspective. Best preparation for that? Tears for your sins.

More happy thoughts.

Dump the earthly entertainments you revel in.

Everywhere you look, the world is full of danger. Head for the desert.

Be a pilgrim traveler. Yes, you're in exile; that's why you should be moaning and groaning about your sins. No wonder you're like the apostle Paul. In his epistle to the Philippians, he wanted to put an end to this life as soon as possible and enter the heavenly kingdom to be with Christ (1:23).

Hate this world and the things that can attract you to sin. That's a protection against the many dangers that will draw an unsuspecting and indeed unwilling person like yourself to hell. What to do? Find Elias and flee with him to the desert; help him found his monastery.

Keep your eyes peeled day and night. Temptations are slipping through the lines. Pray the prayer of Elias. "I've had enough of this life, Lord; I'm ready to move on" (VUL 3 Kings 19:4; NRSV 1 Kings 19:4).

Why would he say that? Better to die with hope and pass through in grace than to live on, sidestepping the devils day after day. As long as soul and body cling together, you can never be free from sin or temptation, nor can you have certitude about future encounters.

Don't be a clown! Don't simper about how long a life you're going to live! And don't think that keeping a long list of *To Dos* will guarantee you a tomorrow!

Remember, a nobleman-cum-millionaire surrounded by all his goods will still die and be buried in the ground. And what can his riches buy then?

Today a king lives and sends imperious orders to the farthest parts of his kingdom; tomorrow he's dead as a dodo, packed into the ground, never to be heard from again. To-day people are lining up to bestow medals and decorations on him; tomorrow nobody cares. Today he's magnified out of all proportion; tomorrow he's just another stiff deprived of his riches and honors, his castles and villas.

Today he's someone special, a king from a long line of kings; tomorrow he's food for the vermin and an offense to the nose. He came into the world with no clothes, and like a pauper and an exile he heads toward the tomb.

How do all the pomps and poops of the world end? In death, pain, grieving, and trembling. Nobody escapes this. Prince, pope, cardinal — they all die, and each is succeeded by a person who himself will die.

You, dear brother, can't be certain you'll live the day out. No papal bull can stop death, nor is there enough money in the world to buy one's way out of death.

Often after requesting a favor and after the favor is granted, death comes to call and hauls everything off.

And so it happens that a man retires from Rome poor and naked, which is in sharp contrast to the day he arrived in Rome and presented his credentials to the curia.

Records indicate that many of the fathers of old lived a very long time, and so did their descendants, but for each there came a time to say, *it's time to die.*

"We all die, like water dripping on the earth from which we sprang" (VUL 2 Samuel 14:14; NRSV 2 Kings 14:14).

What your whole life amounts to at the moment of death is a pause, a slowdown, a half stop. Like wind blowing or daylight dawning. We're just passing through, a guest today but gone tomorrow. Like lightning or a blink of the eye. So perish all the kingdoms and dynasties of the earth.

Count all the hours, days, months, years of your life, and tell me where they went. They've passed, yes, but like shadows from the sun, like patterns in the sand.

What's the inevitable conclusion? Nothing is stable or durable for long on this earth; Adam and his progeny are proof of that; they came from the earth, and after their time they returned to it.

Everything is vain and fragile, no matter how decorous or glamorous it may be in this world.

Don't let the spangles and sequins drag you under the bushes.

Things decorated with paint or inlaid with metal or stone — they fade, lose their value, go out of style.

Therefore in every thing you do and wherever you are, whether you're coming or going, remember that death is right around the corner.

Still more happy thoughts. The apostle Paul, as he said in his epistle to the Philippians, wanted to end it all and leave this life to be with Christ (1:23).

This is much better than living longer in the flesh, headed away from God, being flounced on the waves and frightened to death.

Carry Jesus always in your mind and truly love him and pray to him daily, and you'll have faith in the kingdom of heaven.

Wasn't it the evangelist John who said, "Where I am, Father, my minister is there also?" (12:26).

Last of the happy thoughts.

In your last moments you'll hear the sweet voice of God as Matthew recorded it. "Rejoice, good and faithful servant; yes, heaven is in the details; enter into the joy of the Lord" (25:21).

∾∾∾∾∾∾∾

DEATH

Kempis was no stranger to plagues. Of course, he knew the ten Egyptian ones in Exodus. Water to blood; frogs, gnats, flies, anthrax, boils, hail, locusts, darkness, death of firstborns.

And he was no stranger to the pestilence, later known as the bubonic plague, and later still as the black death, that swept across Europe in the middle of the fourteenth century, killing perhaps as many as twenty million people from 1347 to 1350, which amounted to perhaps a third of the population.

The symptoms have been immortalized in the nursery rhyme or jump-rope jingle.

> *Ring around the rosies,*
> *A pocketful of posies.*
> *Ashes, ashes,*
> *We all fall down.*

Innocent enough as the words seem they have dark meanings.

"Ring around the rosies" referred to the rings on the skin surrounding the reproductive organs and later the arms and legs.

"A pocket full of posies" referred to the bunch of flowers in one's pockets, ready to be whipped out and used as a nose freshener when the stench of dead bodies came too near.

"Ashes, ashes" referred to the mass burning of corpses as perhaps the best way to clear the streets and cure the disease.

"We all fall down" referred to the sad fact that sick people were roaming the streets and dropping dead right on the cobbles.

Still a lovely song for tots who needn't know the subtext, and still a painful reminder to adults of the horrible plague that once was.

The villain whose identity was unknown to medieval medicine? A sick flea living on a black rat.

A hundred years later, in Kempis's own monastery, there was always a monk in the infirmary with symptoms of the disease.

In Kempis's works — *Imitation, Consolations (Soliloquy of a Soul), Meeting the Master in the Garden (Rose and Lilies)* — death is ever present. Physical death, yes, but also spiritual death, of which there are two types: death to all the spiritual things in this life, and death to all the worldly things in this life.

Here in *Meeting the Master in the Garden,* he speaks of death in "Listening" (*Roses, #2*) and "Facing Uncertain Death" (*Lilies, #25*).

As for *The Imitation of Christ* here's what Kempis had to say.

"Death is approaching more quickly than life's unfolding. Think about that now, and put more shoulder into your reformation of life. We're on the near side of death now, but on the far side await the pains of hell or purgatory. Weigh that in your heart, and maybe now you'll be willing to undertake the laborious program of reform, readying yourself for the final rigor" (39).

As for *Consolations for My Soul (Soliloquy of a Soul)* here's what Kempis had to say.

"Just thinking of my last day, my last hour, I turn to jelly! It's too late to pray. It's time to be judged. Everyone gets the justice he or she deserves. *O God so holy, God so strong, don't despair of me! Don't hand me over to a bitter death! Instead, give me a decent place of penance where I can weep quietly over my sins. The last thing I want is to be dismissed from the Light"* (41).

In the end, for Kempis, the worst plague wasn't bubonic. "The worst plague is vainglory, that's to say, the wish to be praised by externs. It's a hollow sort of thing. A sign of pride. Contrary to the grace of God" (*Lilies*, 31). —W.G.

26

Deferring Everything to God

Praise the Lord!
(Psalm VUL 145:2; NRSV 146:1)

Praise the Lord, my soul. Every good has proceeded from him and will now remain with him in eternity. To him, the principle and end of all good, you should defer everything. You should praise him warmly, thankfully, and eventually his consolations will flow again; the font of perennial life will flood the plains.

There's nothing better for you to do than love and praise the most high God.

I say these roses, these lilies, a hundred times over, and I'll repeat them a thousand times more.

There's no study more elegant, no work more eminent, than to love and praise God, creator and redeemer. Do this as long as you live, feel, think.

Work on making progress in what you do and say, day and night, morning noon and night, every hour, every moment, whether you feel like it or not.

Cling always, but only to God, that God may be all things in all things, before all things, above all things, loved, blessed, praised, and exalted by you during the present age.

Do this, and you'll do well with him in the end.

So, faithful soul, exult in the Lord your God. The blessed virgin Mary did much the same thing when she exulted in Jesus her salvation, if I may paraphrase Luke (1:47).

Exult and praise your God who made and redeemed you. You're a debtor of God's, the recipient of daily favors gathered gladly for you. For all this you'll never be able to thank God enough, even if you were an angel. No, you have to thank him as a mere human, never having enough of God's mercy, having to continually implore and ask for more.

Don't stop praying and praising even though you often fall, sin, and offend. Not that you should become desperate about it, more that you should humble yourself when you pray.

Love and be loved. Love purges, heals, makes changes. It turns on and fires up; it scatters sadness to the winds and gives birth to joy of heart, not the sort of joy the world enjoys, not the flesh and blood the world puts a high price on.

Praise God, and you'll be praised. Bless him, and you'll be blessed. Sanctify him, and you'll be sanctified. Magnify him, and you'll be magnified; glorify him, and you'll be glorified by him in body and soul.

But when will this time come, Lord? When will you fill my mouth with perpetual praise? When will my heart exult? When will my heart jump for joy with your saints in your glory?

How long?

Just a little longer, and you'll see great and wonderful things when the final trump sounds.

Then I'll give you to my saints, for all the labor and dolor you'll receive final rest and eternal life. What more would you want? Nothing really, if I may answer my own question. You alone are enough for me, dear God. You give eternal life to your praisers and appraisers. An immense reward for just a little effort. A great reward for the sick. A lasting reward for a few passing efforts on your part.

Give yourself and all you have to God. Give him whatever you do, and have the strength to do.

Paul said much the same thing in his second epistle to the Corinthians. Make it seem that you have nothing of your own. Why? Because you possess everything in God (6:10).

Lord God, you see my face, but I can't see yours. When will you rejoice with me in your kingdom with the clearest possible view of your face?

Light of lights, when will you scatter all the shadows of my life?

True peace, high beatitude, perfect felicity, when will you remove all the obstacles from my heart?

When will I follow you, no potholes, no detours, wherever you go, dear Lord?

When will I see you with my eyes? No more mirrors, No more enigmas, no more parables, no more metaphors, no more questions, no more doubts? No more opinions, no more quizzing by teachers!

When will I know for sure all the things I believe in the Sacred Scriptures and read in various books and hear from readers in many different places?

Will I learn it from my God, from the angels and the choirs of angels, from the glory and beatitude of the celestial homeland, from the peace and joy of the citizens above?

When will I be there? When will I come and appear in your presence? When will I gaze on your joyful face and the glory in your kingdom with the cherubim and seraphim and all the saints?

Alas, that hour hasn't come. I'm on one side of the door of my cell, and you're on the other. There I'll be, dear God, with weepy eyes and drooling mouth, until you come to me.

27

Singing with the Saints and Angels

Within earshot of angels I'll psalm you a psalm.
(Psalm 137:1)

God, king, creator! Laudable and applaudable!

The longer I dally on earth, the farther away I travel from you and your holy angels.

What a pauper and unhappy camper I am! As long as I eat bread on earth — that's to say, the bread of labor and dolor — the more I'll deprive myself of the bread of angels, which contains an eternity of tastes.

Lord, I hear the sound of your praise from the mouths of angels in heaven. It's the same voice John the apostle heard while he was in exile. The voice of many angels psalming as one. "Holy, holy, holy!" (VUL Apocalypse 4:8; NRSV Revelation 4:8.

Would that I were one of them and had such a voice! How I'd serenade you as though you could pick out my voice! How I'd crank out the heavenly song, proclaiming your holy name forever!

Cherubim and seraphim! How sweetly and beautifully, fervently and excellently, you sing and carry on in the presence of God. No tedium, just Te Deum.

After that angelic sound every human sound is raucous; every song, out of synch; every psalm, dull; every piece of music, funereal; all stringed instruments, out of tune; every organ, mute; every worldly joy, a big disappointment; every dramatic presentation, an unholy howl; all food and drink, flat; all flesh, fetid and putrid; all wine, acid and acrid; all honey, poisonous; every pleasantry, a disaster; every decoration, in poor taste; every ornament, tacky; every honor and glory, a curl of smoke; everything precious and noble, cheap and amateurish.

To sum up, all these things have no comparison with eternal life, glory, joy in the sight of God and angels, co-praisers of the Trinity without end.

Alas, I can't ascend to that height of song nor do I comprehend it fully. So I have to content myself with thumping and thwacking my breast, bending my knees before God and man, and humbly asking for forgiveness.

True, my own accomplishments without your grace and mercy, Lord, are fit only for the trashery. But your accomplishments are simply out of this world. "What a treasury of wisdom and knowledge God has to draw on!" wrote Paul to the Romans. "How profound and true his judgments are!" (11:33).

He presides over the good and bad, the grateful and ungrateful, the pious and impious. Yes, everyone has to pass through his court. Why? No other court can investigate your case as thoroughly as his. No last minute surprises in his court!

To that end, all blessings always on God, my God.

28

Praying for Help

Lord, may my prayer arise like incense in your presence.

(Psalm VUL 140:2 NRSV 141:2)

A prayer.

*Lord God of mine, I praise you with all your saints and crea-
tures in every place and time. I bless you and spread the news
about you. I love you always, with pure heart. I magnify and
exalt your holy name above all your holy works.*

*Yes, you're my God, and I'm your poor servant. You're my light
and my hope. My fortitude and my patience. My praise and my
glory. My wisdom and my prudence. My beauty and my sweetness.
My music and my musical instrument. My pipe organ and my
kettledrum. My psalm and my hymn. My incantation and my
jubilation. My helmet and my shield. My bow and my sword.
My gold and my silver — to pay off my debt to you, dear God.*

*You're my tent and my palace. My shield and my banner. My
tower of fortitude and my defender of life. My garden and my
orchard. My greenhouse and my root cellar. My ascetory and my
refectory. My food and my drink.*

*You're my cinnamon and my balsam. My balm and my bath
oils. My rose and my lily. My garland and my crown. My bed and
my cot. My hot tub and my hot towel. My light and my lamp.*

My candelabrum and my constellation. My book inside and my Scripture outside — my Bible in which your total Sacred Scripture lies. My lord and my God. My lecturer and my instructor. My doctor and my apothecary.

In you I find everything and have everything, what with your having donated all of it to me. Beyond that, I find little or nothing of interest.

Therefore, open my heart in your holy law and clear the way for my heart to run. "Return to me the joy of your salvation," as the Psalmist sang out, "I want to hear it in your own words" (VUL 50:14; NRSV 51:12). Why? Because there's no one else to help. No one else to save me and no one else to lead me to eternal life, except you.

Hear me, dear God, when I pray, in sadness as well as gladness, in sickness as well as health. In all these things I commend myself to you, and I bless you forever.

Amen.

29

Uniting with God

Rest up for now, my soul;
the Lord has done you a favor.

(Psalm VUL 114:7; NRSV 116:7)

God is your rest and your peace, your life, salvation, beatitude. So, always defer back to the praise of God all the good things you do, see, and hear. That'll leave the way to your own personal peace and good conscience.

You flourish, but not in yourself and certainly not in others, only in God alone. He gives everything, runs everything, for entirely his own reasons. What can I do? Everything. That's to say, no person or thing, large or small, can hold you back from God.

Perhaps this course of action isn't for you. Or perhaps it is for you, but you can't see yourself doing a great deal. But, you know, it's not impossible to do the whole thing for God. He can unite the devout soul to himself anytime he wants. What's more, he can do it in a flash. All you have to do is forget, erase, expunge everything else from your mind and soul. Then you'll find yourself united to him alone, aflame with the fire of his love, turned into jelly in a jar.

A prayer.

My God, love of my life, I want to stop my pilgrimage, my wandering from one thing to another! When will I be totally united to you with all my strength?

May every creature be silent in your presence. May you alone speak to me, be present to me, illumine me. You are, if I may paraphrase Paul in his first epistle to the Corinthians, the one who gave your eternal blessing on all the torches below and all the chandeliers above (15:28).

If you felt desolate but have been consoled by the Lord, then you may consider yourself a very happy person indeed. You may even find in yourself some decidedly good characteristics that may have escaped you but are well known to the angels.

A living reproach to the bad, but a fine example to the good.

Despised by the proud, befriended by the humble.

Isolated from the worldly, crowded by the spiritual.

A source of amusement to the magnates, a source of honor to the regular folk.

Looking dead on the outside, but very much alive on the inside.

Afflicted by the diseases of the flesh, blessed by the gifts of the spirit.

Physically weak, but mentally strong.

A plain face, but a beautiful conscience.

Worn out by labor, yet invigorated by prayer.

Stooped from carrying your spiritual burdens, but stiffened by consolation.

Tethered to the world, but your spirit has been snatched by God and joined to Christ.

If you have Jesus and Mary and all the angels and saints as friends, you're a happy person in this life. Why? Because they're a motley crew.

Tour guides on the road, councilors in doubt, teachers during study, readers at table, companions in the monastery, friends in conversation, choristers in chant, sentinels in enemy territory, reinforcements in battle, defenders against the enemy, intercessors for sinners, emergency helpers as you lay dying, comforters in your final agony, advocates at the judgment seat, patrons in God's court, movers and shakers in heaven.

Now that you've left the world of your parents and joined this religious order of devout brothers, you now belong to a larger family. God in heaven as your father. Angels as friends. Religious as relatives. All the faithful as neighbors. Old men as uncles. Young men as brothers. Wives as mothers. Virgins as sisters. Paupers as nephews. Pilgrims as cousins. The meek and humble as models. The sober and chaste as dinner companions. The sickly as family. The afflicted and oppressed as housemates. The despicable as amicable companions. Co-conspirators against the world as co-heirs of the heavenly kingdom.

Quite a family! This is the holy generation and noble progeny, born of God, pleasing to God, founded in faith, stiffened by hope, smartened with charity, armed with patience, proven by fire, firmed up by constancy.

30

Seeking True Peace

Peace, I'm here, no need to be afraid.

(Luke 24:36)

Your salvation and peace consist in Christ Jesus. Love him, and you'll have peace and quiet. Above him and beyond him you needn't search for anything more.

What's the peace the faithful soul finds? Peace of soul to bear adversities for the love of God. If you think otherwise, you're sadly mistaken.

Put God first in everything you do, or you'll just be spinning your wheels; half measures won't do.

There's no peace for the impious, the Lord says, but there's no shortage of peace for those who love his law.

The peace Christ taught may be found in a variety of ways. In profound humility, in the abnegation of one's will, in the mortification of every lustful desire, in the rejection of worldly praise and external consolation.

What's the obvious conclusion?

Watch your heart on the inside and all your senses on the outside. Don't fall for the flashy but harmful recreations of the soul.

Creatures are often helpful, though, if they're deferred to the praise of the Creator and the honor of God. Or if they are assumed to have some practical use for self or others. However, beautiful things are often hurtful if their only purpose is to be stared at curiously, naughtily, badly.

The cautious keep a good guard on themselves, but the not-so-cautious are overrun by their vices.

Riches tempt. Money corrupts, delicacies taint, banquets bloat, knowledge inflates, power puffs up, honors elevate. The perverse spit on humble habits; the vain seduce proud souls.

Don't be a fool! The things of this earth do have some practical value, but you must admit they can't satisfy the soul, nor can they produce quiet.

All temporal things are full of defects; without God there's no such thing as perfect, or if there is, there's no way of getting at it.

What's the conclusion of the preceding?

In no living creature or beautiful picture or noble geniture or high stature or great prelature — in none of these put your thought or your desire, that's to say, if you don't want to fall, be trampled on, polluted. Why? That's because the whole earthly enterprise is flashy, slippery, harmful, unless, of course, you draw all things to the source of all good, God himself.

How can you boast of your own holiness? You're still sliding and slipsliding into culpable behavior. You can't stand up on your two spiritual feet? One thing is sure; you shouldn't try to go it alone; you shouldn't ignore others. One thing to do. Offer all good purely and simply to God.

Yes, you'll find peace and quiet in Christ. Yes, you'll be comforted by the sweet and holy word of Christ preached by him on the hill. "Blessed are the clean of heart; they shall see God" (Matthew 5:8).

To whom be praise, honor, glory from every creature forever and ever.

Amen.

31

Relying on God Alone

*If I look up to the Lord, then he'll guide my steps
around the traps below.*

(Psalm VUL 24:15; NRSV 25:15)

In every thought, word, and deed you should always have
right and pure intention to God; that's to say, you should do
everything to the praise and glory and honor of God and the
edification of your neighbor.

He's the cause of all good merits and the grantor of all
eternal rewards.

He ought to be the principle and end of all your works,
that's to say, if you want the fruits of your labors to amount
to anything.

If you recall the memory of the terrible punishments of
God, you'll not boast so vainly about your less-than-holy
activities.

The worst plague is vainglory, that's to say, the wish to be
praised by externs. It's a hollow sort of thing. A sign of pride.
Contrary to the grace of God.

So what are you going to do? Whom can you confide in?
Whom can you rely on? Not in yourself, not in humanity, not
in any particular article in the world, not in the stars of the

sky. But you can rely on God alone, he made you and holds you and the rest of creation in his hand and under his power. The weight of it all means nothing to him; he doesn't have to ask for help.

That's what David psalmed. "My eyes are fixed on the Lord" (VUL 24:15; NRSV 25:15).

Also from David. "Lord, I've made no secret of my joy, and I haven't hid my sorrow" (VUL 37:10; NRSV 38:9).

What's the conclusion?

Now that you've left your planning room behind with all its maps and scrolls, you can run again to the Lord. With some confidence you can bring him all your necessities, even your prayers and holy desires. He's the one who leads you around the hidden traps and snares. Of course, he doesn't want to detour you from the right way of virtue and true humility; only to put you on the main highway to heaven.

Every good deed done for God makes the conscience rejoice, the mind expand, the merits increase.

Every bad deed swamps a good reputation; it impedes the flow of divine grace.

Do something that's vainglorious, and like a gust of wind it'll blow out the flame of your elation. Do something that's worldly, and it'll fall into the mud; that's the clue that God blew his top.

Therefore, you wouldn't rejoice in some felicity of this world, which up to this point has been populated by block-heads. Just stay the course. Fear God. Stay humble.

Should you lapse or fall into error more than you'd like, these humbling experiences will knock you down a few pegs.

You don't want to praise someone to the skies because you don't know what he may be in for in the immediate future.

Suppose someone falls; don't judge him harshly right on the spot. In a flash God can pick the crying fellow up and dust him off.

Pray for everyone. Commit everyone to God.

The smaller you appear in your own eyes, the larger you'll appear in God's eyes.

Respect the humble. Recognize the high and mighty from afar. Don't be the last one to pay your respects.

If others don't think much of you and pass you over for promotion, shed a tear perhaps, but don't boo-hoo for long. Why? Because it's better and more secure to be humbled with the meek and mild than to be reproved by God with the rich and famous.

Avoid being praised, fear being lionized, blush to be honored, flee to be thought a hotshot, try to lay low.

Choose to spend time with God. Rummage around the Scriptures. Take your time while praying.

There's no one who can live without praise and honor, except the one who chooses God over praises and honors.

There's no one who can live without divine solace, except perhaps the person who regards all the joys of the world as nothing, and who shoulders all the contraries of the world for Christ, and who daily desires to be with him in heaven.

32

Doing the Best I Can

I've raised my soul to you, O Lord,
who lives in the heavens.
(Psalm VUL 24:1; NRSV 25:1)

A prayer.

*O Lord God, who keeps a judgmental eye in heaven and on
earth with angels, humans, and other creatures.*

*I can't offer you great lauds and gratifications, which you richly
and justly deserve. I can offer you only the tribs and troubs of my
heart as proof of my contrition for my sins.*

*Do me a favor. Convert every bad of mine into good, and
every good into better. That too for the glory of your name and
the eternal salvation of my soul.*

*Bad, that you should know my clumsiness, my ignorance, my
instability on a daily basis, and you know that every now and
then I turn tail and run for the hills.*

Mercifully spare me, Lord, and mercifully fetch me back to you.

*Put my heart into your presence when I pray and meditate day
and night, as much as my fragile body can do.*

*I want to calm your countenance by bringing you sacred gifts
and prayers. Especially do I want to present to you the three*

pathetic pennies of a poor bloke like myself. Contrition of the heart. Confession of the mouth. Satisfaction of the humble deed.

Lord God of mine, great and lovable. Remember, I'm just a poor pauper. I'm not an angel or a saint. I'm not a great sinner or an innocent lamb. I'm not particularly fervent when it comes to contemplation. And so my service to you hasn't been worthy or worthwhile. I don't deserve to be numbered or named among the devout.

My beloved Lord. May my humble prayer and bitter contrition be acceptable to you. It's not in place of the jubilation of angels or the Gregorian chant of saints. But it's the best I can do.

Nevertheless, I don't despair and I won't despair concerning your forgiveness and mercy; even though I fall too often and am depressed by my own infirmity.

No, I don't shrink and I won't shrink from praising you in my life. Quite the contrary, I shall praise and magnify you, dear God, until the day comes when I arrive in heaven.

I'll praise you always and love you above all things. You, the greatest felicity of angels and saints in the celestial homeland.

33

Keeping Good Company

Seek God, and your soul will live.

(Psalm VUL 68:33; NRSV 69:32)

Nothing better, nothing happier for the soul than this passage from the psalms! But at the end, life's end, there'll be nothing to possess. Maybe you'll want to have a good companion to hold your hand. But who are the good companions, and where do you find them?

Luke suggests the baby Jesus in the crib with the shepherds (2:10). Matthew likes the Holy Magi (2:11). Luke is fond of Simeon and Anna in the temple (2:27–28) or Martha in her town house (10:33). John offers Mary Magdalene at the tomb (20:1). Luke comes up with the apostles in the upper room waiting with great joy for the Holy Spirit (Acts 1:13).

Blessed is the person who seeks Jesus and the other saints, not in a bodily way, but in a spiritual way.

Blessed the person who conducts a detailed and continuous search for Jesus in every time and place, and longs for a clear vision of him, and prepares himself today for that happy event.

Blessed the one who follows Jesus in his life through the passion and cross. He'll be with Jesus as he lays dying, and he won't have to worry about getting a bad outcome to the final judgment. He'll see not only Jesus but also the disciples of Jesus and all those who love him and patiently bear adversities because of what he did first.

Love of Jesus and his friends spurns the world and repels every vain and impure thought.

Therefore, leave behind your earthly friends and acquaintances — anyone who can get in the way of your solitude and devotion.

When you need some solace in the privacy of your own cell, call on the saints, apostles, and relatives of Jesus. They'll speak to you about the kingdom of God and the state of beatitude. They'll tell you how your many tribulations are just so many cobbles on the bumpy road to companionship with them.

Make a visit, albeit a mystical visit, to the saints and holy citizens, to the celestial court, to the secret tabernacle, to the oratory of blessed Mary the virgin, far removed from the crowds of the world. Seek there some solace for your soul, and don't lessen your prayer time until you get there.

Overhear the angel of the Lord speaking with Mary about the incarnation of Christ and the redemption of humankind (Luke 1:28–37).

If you can find the time, spend it with the angel Gabriel and the blessed virgin Mary, eavesdropping on their discussion of the celestial mysteries.

Believe most firmly that all the news committed to Mary is true; as Mary believed God and the angel were sent to her from heaven, so should you.

Then look around for St. John the Baptist, precursor of our Lord Jesus Christ, hiding out as a hermit, with bended knees greet him most devoutly.

"Hello, John, most holy and beloved friend of Jesus Christ! I've heard good things about you, how your pregnancy and birth was something of a miracle itself, how you became a solitary lest you commit a sin by the thought of hunger."

Do what you have to do to stay with him. Find out what he ate and drank, and who brought the food to him, whether his father or mother sent some stuff, and, if so, when did they do it, whether he ever left the desert to go back to them for a visit, whether the holy angel Gabriel descended to him and revealed secrets to him, whether Jesus personally appeared to him and offered his hand in comfort; that's what Luke wrote in his gospel, "the hand of the Lord was with him" (1:66).

Whichever questions you choose to ask John, commit it totally to the Holy Spirit, which filled, taught, and ruled him, adorned his whole life with virtues, looked after him in the hermitage, watched over him in his public and prison life, and finally received his soul with the palm of martyrdom.

Next, proceed to the apostles of Christ. Ask for Peter; go with him to the temple to pray, and climb the stairs to the upper room to receive the Holy Spirit.

Look up Paul in Damascus or Ephesus; make your way with him to the place where he preached the gospel of Christ not in body but in spirit.

Look at how he labors harder than the others and prays as often as they do, and how frequently he's rapt up in prayer and contemplation (2 Corinthians 12:2).

Flying with the sublimes — that's to say, ecstasy — that's not given to everybody, yet he had this to say as he was descending from the heights. "I don't think I understand what just happened to me" (Philippians 3:13).

After the unusual prayer experience, Paul instructed the humble in life in the passion of Christ. "Knowing as much as I do about you Corinthians is nice," he wrote in his first epistle to them, "but Jesus Christ and him crucified is all I need to know" (2:2).

Follow Paul, and he'll lead you on the right road to Christ and through the cross to heaven.

Look around and ask for Andrew, the apostle who preached Christ in parts of Achaia. Listen to his words as he hangs upside down on the cross for the name of Christ.

Next you might want to look up James Major; he suffered and was killed by Herod. Drink with him the chalice of the passion by patiently tolerating pains for the love of God and the salvation of your soul.

Moving right along, look for John, the apostle Jesus loved; he was sent into exile for the name of Jesus. On an island, filled with divine revelation from on high, he wrote with figures of speech and mystical words the last book of the New Testament about the state of the church militant and church triumphant. After these, for the erudition of all the churches and faithful, he published the last gospel about the divinity of Christ.

Read and study these and other books of Scripture, and learn from them about your own capture and the consolation of your exile in this world, not that you be seen as learned and wise, but rather as meek and patient, mild and obedient all the way to death.

Then seek out the other holy apostles who spent their lives for your consolation in Christ's service, those martyred for faith in and love of Christ, and the many others whose words and examples have been edifying.

Visit James, brother of the Lord and writer of the canonical epistle bearing his name; it contains the outline of Christian life and religious perfection.

Find Thomas who spent the last part of his life in India; he reverently touched the wounds of Christ before his faith firmed up, and with fervent love openly cried out, as John recorded it. "My Lord and my God!" (20:28).

Put high on your must-see list a visit to the saintly and erudite apostle, Matthew, the evangelist who wrote in Hebrew the gospel of Christ addressed to the whole world and leading them to salvation.

In a similar manner and with the same affection, look up the other saintly apostles and disciples of Jesus Christ who taught the people to maintain the word of God in their own countries; all of them labored in the vineyard of the Lord until their deaths.

These are the saints and friends of God, by combining the blood of martyrs with the crown of martyrdom, they deserved eternal life.

Summing up, I suggest you read freely about their lives and passions; that's the best consolation for you in your own labors and dolors. That's because nothing you do and suffer for Christ in the service of God will surpass the saints and other devouts.

GUARDIAN ANGELS

In chapter 13 and 18 of *Lilies,* Kempis makes mention of a "holy angel" coming to a monk in need, that's to say, a guardian angel. Perhaps a word about such a celestial being is in order here. I quote from an essay, "Guardian Angel," by Hugh Pope (*Catholic Encyclopedia,* 7:49–50).

That every individual soul has a guardian angel has never been defined by the Church and is, consequently, not an article of faith; but it is the "mind of the Church," as St. Jerome expressed it. "How great the dignity of the soul, since each one has from his birth an angel commissioned to guard it!"

This belief in guardian angels can be traced throughout all antiquity, pagans like Menander and Neo-Platonists like Plotinus held it. It was also the belief of the Babylonians and Assyrians, as their monuments testify.

In the Bible this doctrine is clearly discernible, and its development is well marked. In Genesis angels not only act as the executors of God's wrath against the cities of the plain, but they deliver Lot from danger (28–29), in Exodus an angel is the appointed leader of the host of Israel (12–13), and God says to Moses: "My angel shall go before thee" (32:34).

At a much later period we have the story of Tobias, which might serve for a commentary on the words of Psalm 90:11: "For he hath given his angels charge over thee; to keep thee in all thy ways" (cf. Psalm 33:8 and 34:5). Lastly, in Daniel angels are entrusted with the care of particular districts, one is called "prince of the kingdom of the Persians," and Michael is termed "one of the chief princes" (10; cf. Deuteronomy 32:8 [Septuagint]; and Ecclesiasticus 17:17 [Septuagint].

This sums up the Old Testament doctrine on the point; it is clear that the Old Testament conceived of God's angels as his ministers who carried out his behests, and who were at times given special commissions, regarding men and mundane affairs. There is no special teaching; the doctrine is rather taken for granted than expressly laid down (2 Machabees 3:25; 10:29; 11:6; 15:23).

But in the New Testament the doctrine is stated with greater precision. Angels are everywhere the intermediaries between God and man, and Christ set a seal upon the Old Testament teaching. "See that you despise not one of these little ones: for I say to you, that their angels in heaven always see the face of my Father who is in heaven" (Matthew 18:10).

A twofold aspect of the doctrine is here put before us: even little children have guardian angels, and these same angels lose not the vision of God by the fact that they have a mission to fulfil on earth.

Without dwelling on the various passages in the New Testament where the doctrine of guardian angels is suggested, it may suffice to mention the angel who succored Christ in the garden and the angel who delivered St. Peter from prison. Hebrews puts the doctrine in its clearest light. "Are they not all ministering spirits, sent to minister for them, who shall receive the inheritance of salvation." (1:14). This is the function of the guardian angels; they are to lead us, if we wish it, to the kingdom of heaven.

Complementing the above is this from the *New Catholic Encyclopedia*: "The concept of guardian angel as a distinct spiritual being sent by God to protect every man is a development of Catholic theology and piety not literally contained in the Bible but fostered by it" (T. L. Fallon, *New Catholic Encyclopedia*, 1:519).

Here's what *The Revell Bible Dictionary* says about the nature of angels: "The Bible leaves many questions about angels unanswered. The occasional references give us clues as to their nature, but there is still much we must deduce for ourselves" (63).

And it might be good here to distinguish the traditional idea of such angels with the modern ones. In our time angels abound in movies, television shows, and novels. Few may be considered divine angels; most are secular, freelance, Lone Ranger–type messengers sent by movie, television, novel writers with special, sometimes emergency, messages. Most are well meaning, but a few are menacing. Always remember that, for good or ill, they're fictional. —W.G.

34

Wandering and Squandering

I'll be satisfied only when I see you face to face.

(Psalm VUL 16:15; NRSV 17:15)

A prayerful question.

Dear Lord, how can a person arrive at this glory?

A prayerful answer.

Through contempt of self and all earthly things, and through ardent love of all celestial goods.

Witnesses that it works are the souls of saints rejoicing in the kingdom of heaven; witnesses also are the faithful in their daily fight against the temptations of vices.

From this, from eternally enjoying the glorious end and summum bonum there are those who put a good distance between them. The proud demons and pagan infidels, the perverse Jews and obstinate heretics, carnal men who love the world and neglect God: constituencies all who find felicity only in earthly goods and honors and praises.

Alas, dear God, there are those who run, labor, strive to have and acquire all these earthly goods, and almost never sleep; they don't stop the solicitation process until they acquire something.

When they do acquire something whether rightly or indirectly they're still not content. They want to climb higher and lord it over the rest and feel a sense of pride in the wonderfulness of themselves. They cast themselves as learned gents, think themselves as gentlemen of distinction, give the impression of having been honored by others.

And nevertheless the whole earthly thing is flashy, slippery, nothing to write home about, and finally what they're lusting for is deadly dangerous.

Certainly you have wandered and squandered yourselves in things the world counted as sweet and happy in the present life. That's because you have no certainty concerning all your goods even as you're fast approaching death and God's impending judgment.

For there's nothing in this life so happy as having some measure of bitter sorrow, nothing so precious that can satisfy the human soul, rescue from every evil, refill with every good, and gladden at any moment — except God alone, the highest good, eternal, immense.

This is the creator of all visible things and all invisible things and of human beings. He's before all things and above all things and in all things, dear God, blessed forever.

I mean, what decent worthwhile thing can be said about God or thought about by any creature in heaven or earth? God exceeds everything; in his eyes everything appears null and void.

So every soul is silly if it seeks stuff outside God and loves the things that separate the mind from the love and honor of God.

Great and wonderful are your works, O Lord; to recognize and evaluate each and every one is no job for a creature.

What therefore shall I do? I can't climb the mountain-top, and I can't penetrate the secrets of heaven, nor can I contemplate the face of my God as angels do.

I confess myself unworthy to enjoy any of these great goods or to converse with the saints in heaven.

So my last resort is to humble myself and despise myself in the presence of God and man for as long as I live. I'll be vile in my own eyes so that God will have mercy on me from now on.

As the prophet Isaiah said, "I shall rethink all my years in the bitterness of my soul for which I merited his wrath" (38:15).

A little moaning, a little groaning, and I'll calm the God I offended so often in words and deeds, by my eyes and ears and all the rest of my senses. He gave them to me and expected me to guard them in my whole heart for as long as I'll live.

I shouldn't despair or feel crestfallen when I mess up. Instead I should recall all your good things, and all your mercies until with the help of your grace I deserve to arrive at your salvation. Free me from all sudden evils; more often than not they distract the heart down from meditating on celestial goods.

Be present to me, pious God, and put me next to you, lest I begin to wander and squander the summum bonum, which, of course, is you, Lord. For my whole good is in you alone. Give yourself to me, Lord God, and my soul will have enough once and for all, that's to say, my salvation.

THUS ENDS
VALLEY OF LILIES

Afterword

Who Was Kempis?
Who Owns Kempis?
How to Read a Kempis Book
Kempis and the Bible
Devotio Moderna
Translation, Literal or Paraphrasal

Who Was Kempis?

He was himself, of course, but in time he became several others. Thomas Haemerken was born 1379–80 in Kempen, a village near Düsseldorf in what was then the Rhineland. His father was a blacksmith and his mother something of a schoolmistress.

In 1393, following his older brother's footsteps, he left his country home and went to the city of Deventer. For a while he stayed at the house of Florent Radewijns; he took Thomas under his wing and indeed under his roof, as he had the older brother John Haemerken ten years before.

There he may have met Gerard Groote, founder of a small faith community called, for want of a better name, Brothers of the Common Life. It was a ragtag crowd, made up mostly of laypeople who wanted more, much more of everything spiritual, than they were able to get in the local churches.

Some of the regulars — perhaps I should say "irregulars" since "regulars" meant vowed to a religious rule or ruler, like a bishop — had jobs and families and came at night for the spiritual refreshment. Others lived in the house, kept their day jobs, contributed to a common purse. Odd thing, though. No vows or promises, no attempt to formalize this loosey-goosey group into a religious community under the protection and indeed inspection of the local bishop.

In 1399 Thomas moved uphill to the monastery of St. Agnes, where there was a community of Augustinians. There he entered the religious order, where his brother John was now prior. He was ordained there in 1413 and died there in 1471.

But long before his death Thomas found himself at the gate of heaven. That's to say, at the doorway to the *scriptorium* where the Augustinians earned enough income to survive by copying manuscripts, sacred as well as profane. In this happy room, amid pots of inks and piles of writing materials, was a whole publishing enterprise. In it Kempis was said to have copied, among many other works, the Latin Vulgate Bible of St. Jerome four times.

As for the Brothers and indeed the Sisters of the Common Life downhill, he never really left them. That's to say, he serviced them as well as his own community as spiritual director, novice master, sub prior. Most of his life, however, he spent in the writing room-cum-library — and that's where he assumed at least two additional identities.

Thomas archived the works of Groote and Radewijns and others, however loosely connected with the group. He used their materials for his own edification first and then the edification of others. He even incorporated their works into his own. One of them was *The Imitation of Christ*. That's to say, he ordered their works, edited them, took extracts from them for inclusion in anthologies like the *Imitation*.

The *Imitation* had been widely circulated before someone thought to put Kempis's name on the title page. Apparently, he didn't complain. But it really represented the reality that, whenever he preached or wrote, Groote and Radewijns, though long dead, were ever at his elbow.

Hence, when one speaks of Thomas Haemerken as an author, one includes Groote and Radewijns and perhaps others, whether one knows it or not.

Who Owns Kempis?

At least one good thing came out of the Reformation and Counter-Reformation. Both sides claimed Kempis as their exclusive possession. Fortunately, he didn't have to choose sides, what with his having died some hundred years before the Wittenberg Door.

Today, Kempis is gratefully remembered by Catholics, Protestants, and Evangelicals alike as author of *The Imitation of Christ*, a Vade Mecum, Baedeker, Michelin, Fodor, Zagat guide to the Soul, on the tearful yet joyful trudge that is the Christian pilgrimage. Those who've been looking after their own souls or indeed the souls of others have relied on it for almost six centuries.

He lived in the fifteenth century, a time when Catholicism flourished. There wasn't a great deal to be ecumenical about then. Protestantism and Evangelicalism had yet to come down the pike. But in the twenty-first century there are some passages of what we would call today pure ecumenism.

As an illustration, I pick some paragraphs from the fourth book of the *Imitation*. Dealing as it does with the Blessed Sacrament, it hasn't been read by most Protestant and Evangelicals. But in chapter 11 may be found this striking ecumenical appeal.

My body's a prison, and the view from my cell is grim. I survive, but barely. I do without things in this wretched state, but two things I just can't live without. Food and Light. And you, dear Lord, you bring them to me in the middle of the night.

Food? Your Sacred Body, which revives my sagging mind and body.

Light? Your Divine Word. As the Psalmist has sung in similar circumstances, it's a lamp for my shackled feet (VUL 118:105; NRSV 119:105).

Without the Food and without the Light I wither. Without the Bread and without the Bible I wander. Without the Sacrament of Life and the Book of Life, I perish.

From my cell I see — or think I see — an altar. A Holy Table from which rises Holy Church in all her splendor. On one side is the Holy Bread, that's to say, the precious Body of Christ. On the other, the Holy Bible, that's to say, the Divine Law that contains Holy Doctrine, teaches right faith, leads even the imprisoned soul through the veil of veils to the Holy of Holies, as the Letter to the Hebrews has led us to expect (6:19).

Food and Light, Bread and Bible, Body of Christ and Holy Bible — Kempis said he couldn't live without both to sustain him. And we, Christians of every stripe, would do well to follow his example.

In addition to remembering the *Imitation,* Catholics, Protestants, and Evangelicals may now remember Kempis for his *Consolations, Roses,* and *Lilies.*

Kempis and the Bible

Thomas à Kempis (1379/80–1471) is acknowledged as a spiritual master today, but for centuries his reputation was tarnished by the charge that in his works he quoted the Bible few times and, hence, couldn't have known all that much about the Book of Books, which contained all that needed to be known.

Actually, just the opposite is true. He was a copyist by profession, making during his long and full life four hand-written copies of the complete Bible, including what's referred to today as the Apocrypha.

When his *Opera Omnia* (Complete Works) were published in seven volumes (1902–22), included in the back matter of each volume was a list of Scripture verses quoted or alluded to. In the *Imitation,* for example, Kempis made at least a thousand such references. Most were allusions, that's to say, a play on the words of each reference as it suited the particular Kempis context.

(In addition to the scriptural authors, Kempis also quoted, often not citing the source, such classical Greek and Latin authors as Aristotle, Seneca, Ovid, Virgil, Cicero, Lucan, and Dionysius.)

What Bible did Kempis use?

In the fourth century Pope Damasus (A.D. 366–84) asked his talented secretary Jerome if he wouldn't take on the humongous task of harmonizing the Latin Bible texts and rendering the whole into Latin for a lowbrow audience (Vulgate), that would match the lowbrow Greek Bible (Koine) And so he did.

Not only did Kempis copy the Vulgate Bible professionally, and use it editorially in his books, he also used it devotionally for a lifetime as an Augustinian monk. Hence, his knowledge of the Bible may be said to be intimate, biblical quotations and allusions running through his works like golden threads. For example, in *Consolations for My Soul,* which is half the length of the *Imitation,* he made at least three hundred quotations or allusions; in *Roses,* 50; in *Lilies,* 119.

Please note that in a few recent versions of the *Imitation,* translators have footnoted or endnoted quotations and allusions, and left it at that. In my translations of Kempis, however, rather than doing that, I've inserted each and every allusion into the Kempis text. And in trying to reproduce the flavor of the Latin original, I didn't just resort to plugging in snippets from an approved English translation of the Vulgate (alas, there isn't one at the moment); rather I've translated the original Latin Vulgate texts into my own paraphrasal English and slipped them into the English translation of Kempis without so much as leaving a seam behind. For better or worse.

More about Paraphrase below.

The reader will surely have noticed by now that Scripture sources have been included in the text in parentheses, and they come in three different ways.

First, when Bible book, chapter, and verse are the same in both the Latin Vulgate and the New Revised Standard Version, the Bible versions aren't named.

Second, when the Bible books are the same, but the chapter and verse have different numbers, then both VUL and NRSV are given; for example: (Psalm VUL 7:28; NRSV 7:29).

Third, when the Bible book is the same but has a different name, then both are given; for example, (VUL Book of Wisdom 12:15; NRSV Wisdom of Solomon 12:15).

Please note that references to the New Revised Standard Bible merely indicate where the same sentiment, but not necessarily the same wording, may be found.

Devotio Moderna

Devotio moderna was a reform movement, a renewal movement, a good example of *ecclesia semper reformanda* (a church always renewing itself), the sort of activity that keeps an old entity from becoming an odd entity. Simply put, it felt that the church had lost touch with the people.

The Modern Devotion, as it was called in English, peaked in the fifteenth century and piqued in the sixteenth century the next wave of reformers who, some of them anyway, destroyed the Brethren and Sistern. The levelers too felt that the church had lost touch with the people.

With its roots in the Netherlands, the Modern Devotion spread over much of northern Europe. One hundred houses of the Brethren, three hundred houses of the Sistern. By virtue of the international traffic in manuscripts, especially from one monastery to another, the Modern Devotion spread even farther. In England it quickly came to be thought that the *Imitation* had been written by the author of such thoroughly English works as *The Ladder of Perfection* and *The Cloud of Unknowing.*

From the first short chapter of the First Book (there are four) of the *Imitation,* one can immediately gather the drift of the work and indeed the movement. [The following excerpt is from my paraphrasal translation of the *Imitation* (San Francisco: HarperSanFrancisco, 2000), pp. 3–5.]

Spirit of Pursuit

"The Devout who shadows my every move won't lose me in the dark." At least that's what Christ says, or what the

Evangelist John says Christ said (8:12). He tells us to walk on, through the darkness, with Christ as our only torch. That way, when morning comes, we mayn't have gained a step, but we won't have lost one either. And on into the day we must pursue with doggéd tread the life of Jesus Christ.

Spirit of Christ

We Devouts know more about Christ than we do about the Saints. For example, the Devout who finds the spirit of Christ discovers in the process many "unexpected delights," if I may use an expression of the Apostle John's from the last book of the New Testament (2:17).

But that isn't often the case. Many who've heard the gospel over and over again think they know it all. They've little desire to discover if there's more to the story. That's because, as the Apostle Paul diagnosed it in his letter to the Romans (8:9), "they don't have the spirit of Christ."

On the other hand, the Devout who wants to understand the words of Christ fully and slowly savor their sweetness has to work hard at making himself another Christ.

Vanity of the Knowables

If you're not humble, you make the Trinity nervous, and in that wretched state, what possible good do you get out of standing up in public and disputing to high heaven about the Trinity as an intellectual entity? The real truth, if only you'd learn it, is that hifalutin words don't make a devout a saint. Only a virtuous life can do that, and only that can make God care for us.

Compunction is a good example. The schoolmen at the university could produce lengthy, perhaps even lacy, definitions of this holy word, but that wouldn't move them one inch closer to the gate of heaven. The humble devout, on the other hand, who can neither read nor write, might very well have experienced compunction every day of his life; he's the one, whether he knows it or not, who'll find himself already waiting at that very gate when the final day comes.

Are you any the richer, if I may put it the way Paul did in his First Epistle to the Corinthians (13:3), for knowing all the proverbs of the Bible and all the axioms of the Philosophers, when you're really all the poorer for not knowing the charity and the grace of God?

"Vanity of vanities, and everything is vanity," says the Ancient Hebrew Preacher (Ecclesiastes 1:2). The only thing that isn't vanity is loving God and, as Moses preached to the Israelites, serving him alone (Deuteronomy 6:13). That's the highest wisdom, to navigate one's course, using the contempt of the world as a chart, toward that heavenly port.

Vanity of the Perishables

Just what is vanity? Well, it's many things. A portfolio of assets that are bound to crash. A bird-breast of medals and decorations. A brassy solo before an unhearing crowd. The alley-catting one's "carnal desires," as Paul so lustily put it to the Galatians (5:16), only to discover that punishment awaits further up and farther in. Pining for a long life and at the same time paying no attention to the good life. Focusing both eyes on the present without casting an eye toward the future. Marching smartly in the passing parade instead of falling all over oneself trying to get back to that reviewing stand where Eternal Joy is queen.

Vanity of the Visibles

Don't forget the hoary wisdom of the Ancient Hebrew Preacher. "The eye is never satisfied by what it sees; nor the ears, by what they hear" (Ecclesiastes 1:8). With that in mind, try to transfer your holdings from the visible market into the invisible one. The reason? Those who trade in their own sensualities only muck up their own account and in the process muddy up God's final account.

A caution. Kempis, and indeed the Modern Devotion, has traditionally been thought of as anti-intellectual. But that's far from the truth. Kempis himself was something of an intellectual.

Two points. First, university men, even while dealing with divine topics, often sailed off into the fairyland of the intellect. Second, Systematic Theology wasn't all in the books, except, of course, in the books of the Bible and books of Ascetical Theology (another name for Christian spirituality).

It should be added here that *Devotio Moderna* as a historical movement may have passed away but, through the writings of Kempis and his fellows, especially the *Imitation of Christ*, it has become a *devotio perennis*, that's to say, a devotion for all times, but especially ours.

Translation,
Literal or Paraphrasal

How is it that *Roses* and *Lilies,* written in fifteenth-century Latin, read like twenty-first century English? That's to say, isn't this translation too free, too racy, too irreverent, to be right? Can it possibly represent what must surely have been a fairly dull Latin text?

The answer to the second question is no; to the third, yes. Perhaps some definitions will help.

There are least two theories of translation.

Literal translation, the method favored by academics, strives to be faithful to the Latin text; that's to say, it translates every Latin word into an English word. Denotations only; no connotations. If the Latin sentence has one hundred words, then the English sentence must have at least a hundred words. And so on. Fidelity is the cardinal virtue of literal translation, but sometimes it can turn into a cardinal sin; that's to say, no matter how the literal translator lumbers on, the translated passage may turn out to be more obscure than the Latin.

Paraphrasal translation, on the other hand, has a fidelity of its own, but to the meaning of a Latin passage, not to its wording. Denotations, yes, but connotations too. If the Latin sentence has a hundred words, then the paraphrase will also have a hundred words, but more likely in ten sentences of ten words each; more likely still, it may have ten sentences but perhaps with a word total of two hundred, perhaps even three hundred words.

An illustration, if I may, taken from Kempis's *Imitation of Christ* (book 2, chapter 11).

LATIN	*Multi miracula eius venerantur; pauci ignominiam crucis sequuntur.*
LITERAL	Many venerate his miracles; few follow the ignominy of his cross.
PARAPHRASAL	Many are wowed by his miracles; few are wooed by his cross.

The difference between literal and paraphrasal is remarkable, and indeed desirable.

Some observations on translations.

1. All translations from Latin into English, including this one, good as they may seem, are bound to fail. That's to say, if a translation catches as much as 25 percent of the Latin original, then it's done well.

2. Caution! Paraphrasal translation may convey the meaning of a text well, but it should never be used in school exercises. Scholarship requires that a paraphrasal translation, if used at all, should be used only in conjunction with a literal translation and the Latin original.

3. Paraphrasal translation requires, at the very least, partial mastery of Latin but complete mastery of English. With literal translation by academics, it's the other way round. They're mightily equipped in the foreign, but woefully equipped in the mother, tongue.

Appendix

Kempis's Chapter Titles

ROSES

1. Good Companionship Rather than Bad (1)

2. Flight from the World and the Snares of the Devil (2)

3. True Wisdom in God's Presence (3)

4. Battle against One's Own Vices (4)

5. Acquisition of the Grace of Devotion (5)

6. Hearing and Reading the Divine Sermon / Conversation (6)

7. Divine Consolation in Tribulation (7)

8. The Joy of a Good Conscience in the Holy Spirit (8)

9. Good Habits of a Humble Brother (9)

10. Instability of the Human Heart (10)

11. Trust in God during Hard Times (11)

12. Virtue of Praying and Usefulness of Sacred Reading (12–13)

13. Praise of Charity and Its Fruits (14)

14. Vigilance and Effort against Temptations (15)

15. Fraternal Burden of Each Other (16)

16. Love of Christ and Hate for the World (17)

LILIES

Prolog of the Book Called *Valley of Lilies*

Bibliography

Thomas à Kempis

The Chronicles of the Canons Regular of Mount St. Agnes. Translated by J. P. Arthur. London: Kegan, Paul, Trench, Trübner & Co., 1906.

Consolations for My Soul, Being a translation of "Soliloquy of a Soul." Translated by William Griffin. New York: Crossroad, 2004.

The Founders of the New Devotion, Being the Lives of Gerard Groote, Florentius Radewin and Their Followers. Translated by J. P. Arthur. London: 1905.

The Imitation of Christ. Translated by William Griffin. San Francisco: HarperSanFrancisco, 2000.

A Meditation on the Incarnation of Christ: Sermons on the Life and Passion of Our Lord, and Of Hearing and Speaking Good Words. Translated by Dom Vincent Scully, C.R.L. London: Kegan Paul, Trench & Trübner, 1907.

Meditations on the Life of Christ. Translated and edited by the Venerable Archdeacon Wright and the Rev. S. Kettlewell. With a Preface by the latter. New York: E. P. Dutton, 1892.

Opera Omnia Thomae Hemerken a Kempis. Edited by M. J. Pohl. 7 vols. Freiburg: Herder, 1902–22.

Bibles

Biblia Sacra Juxta Vulgatam Clementinam Divisionibus, Summariis, et Concordantiis Ornata. Parisiis: Desclée et Socii, 1927.

Knox, Ronald A. *The Holy Bible: A Translation from the Latin Vulgate in the Light of the Hebrew and Greek Originals.* New York: Sheed & Ward, 1950.

New Revised Standard Version. *The Holy Bible, containing the Old and New Testaments with the Apocryphal/Deuterocanonical Books.* New York: Oxford University Press, 1989.

Nova Vulgata, Bibliorum Sacrorum Editio.

Reference Works

Achtemeier, Paul J., general editor. *Harper Collins Bible Dictionary.* Rev. ed. San Francisco: HarperSanFrancisco, 1996 (1985).

Butler, Alban, compiler and editor. *Lives of the Saints.* 12 vols. London: Burns and Oates, 1864. *Butler's Lives of the Saints,* second revised and expanded edition by Herbert Thurston; 1930s. Third revised and expanded edition by Donald Attwater, 1956. Reissued in 1980 Westminster, Md.: Christian Classics, 1980.

Diamond, Wilfrid. *Dictionary of Liturgical Latin.* Milwaukee: Bruce, 1961.

Farmer, David Hugh, compiler and editor. *Oxford Dictionary of Saints.* Oxford: Oxford University Press, 1978. 2nd ed., 1987.

Hornblower, Simon, and Antony Spawforth. *The Oxford Classical Dictionary.* 3rd ed. Oxford: Oxford University Press, 1999.

Niemeyer, J. F. *Mediae Latinitatis Lexicon Minus.* Leiden: Brill, 1997.

Richards, Lawrence O., general editor. *The Revell Bible Dictionary.* Old Tappan, N.J.: Fleming H. Revell, 1990.

Souter, Alexander. *A Glossary of Latin to 600 A.D.* Oxford: Clarendon Press, 1996 (1949).

Sources

Butler, D. *Thomas à Kempis: A Religious Study.* London: Anderson & Ferrier, 1908.

Cruise, F. R. *Thomas à Kempis: Notes of a Visit to the Scenes in Which His Life Was Spent.* London: K. Paul, 1887.

Hyma, Albert. *The Brethren of the Common Life.* Grand Rapids, Mich.: Wm. B. Eerdmans, 1950.

————. *The Christian Renaissance: A History of the "Devotio Moderna."* 1st ed. New York, 1925. 2nd ed. Hamden, Conn.: Archon Books, 1965.

Kettlewell, Samuel. *Thomas à Kempis and the Brothers of Common Life.* London: K. Paul, Trench, 1882.

Montmorency, J. E. G. de. *Thomas à Kempis: His Age and His Book.* London: Methuen, 1906.

Scully, Vincent. *Life of the Venerable Thomas à Kempis, Canon Regular of St. Augustine.* With Introduction by Francis Cruise. London: R. & T. Washbourne, 1902.

Van Engen, J., editor. *Devotio Moderna: Basic Writings.* Preface by Heiko A. Oberman. New York: Paulist Press, 1988.

Background

Cantor, Norman F. *The Civilization of the Middle Ages.* "A Completely Revised and Expanded Edition of *Medieval History: The Life and Death of a Civilization.*" New York: HarperCollins, 1993.

————. *In the Wake of the Plague: The Black Death and the World It Made.* New York: Free Press, 2001.

————. *Inventing the Middle Ages: The Lives, Works, and Ideas of the Great Medievalists of the Twentieth Century.* New York: William Morrow, 1991.

————, general editor. *The Encyclopedia of the Middle Ages.* New York: Viking, 1999.

Durant, Will. *The Reformation: A History of European Civilization from Wyclif to Calvin: 1300–1564.* New York: Simon and Schuster, 1957.

Fines, John. *Who's Who in the Middle Ages: From the Collapse of the Roman Empire to the Renaissance.* New York: Barnes & Noble Books, 1970.

Huizinga, Johan. *The Waning of the Middle Ages: A Study of the Forms of Life, Thought, and Art in France and the Netherlands in the*

Dawn of the Renaissance. New York: Doubleday Anchor Books, 1954 (1949, 1924).

Le Goff, Jacques. *Medieval Civilization: 400–1500*. New York: Barnes & Noble Books, 1988 (1964).

Mollat, Michel. *The Poor in the Middle Ages: An Essay in Social History*. Translated by Arthur Goldhammer. New Haven: Yale University Press, 1986 (1978).

Raitt, Jill, with Bernard McGinn and John Meyendorff, editors. *Christian Spirituality: High Middle Ages and Reformation*. World Spirituality 2. New York: Crossroad, 1987.

Tuchman, Barbara W. *A Distant Mirror: The Calamitous 14th Century*. New York: Alfred A. Knopf, 1978.

About the Translator

William Griffin has been an editor in two New York publishing houses (Harcourt and Macmillan), a literary agent in New Orleans (Southern Writers), and a magazine journalist (*Publishers Weekly*). He has done major biographical work on C. S. Lewis, G. K. Chesterton, and Billy Graham. He has anthologized the works of all three and written three novels and a number of short stories.

Recently, with thirteen years of Latin study behind him, he has taken to translating medieval and Renaissance spiritual classics into truly modern English: The *Imitation of Christ* and *Consolations for My Soul* by Thomas à Kempis; *Sermons to the People: Advent, Christmas, New Year's, Epiphany* by Augustine of Hippo; and *Short Shrifts: A Brief Life of Augustine of Hippo in His Own Words*. He was also originator of *Verbum Diurnum,* a Latin Word-for-the-Day on the Internet.

A Word
from the Editor

This is now the third volume in a series of contemporary translations (or paraphrases) by William Griffin of the works of Thomas à Kempis. The first in the series, *The Imitation of Christ*, is one of the most recognized devotional classics in the history of Christian publishing and is available in many formats and forms. It has sold millions of copies around the world for hundreds of years. Bill's version is unique, though, as are the two subsequent volumes. The second and third volumes (the second volume was published by Crossroad under the title *Consolations for My Soul*) had not been available in English for centuries. Bill believed, as I do, that these works deserved to be available in readable and accessible contemporary translations for postmodern readers. It is always a challenge to render works written in archaic and old style English into language that will have some sparkle and contemporary feel to it. Bill has brought his skills to this task and admirably paraphrased the Latin text into a unique devotional style and format.

But it is true that piety in a particular form may not sound like piety to others in a different age. This is, of course, only one of the reasons that we have new translations and paraphrases of the Bible arriving on the scene almost every year. In each case I think the Church is serviced by these new versions and that they do help all of us read the Word of God with new eyes and hear about the biblical experiences in new ways. So I would encourage you to set aside, as you can and as it seems relevant, assumptions about what is pious language and how a saint might express himself (or herself in another case) and just enjoy the ride.

Within this volume, and in the second volume, you can read "asides" about Bill's unique approach to the text and his understanding of what it means to do a contemporary paraphrase. His addition of mini-essays about various background subjects and topics has enhanced this third volume (and the second volume) to the degree that I may boast confidently that you will learn more about this kind of devotional literature, the times in which it was written, and the characters involved than you might have imagined.

But what I also want you to know is that Bill's command and knowledge of the original Latin text is impressive and his own intention in these works is to break out of pious boxes wrought in the language and the thought forms of an earlier time. Not because he is against pietism; he definitely is not. But because he wants you the reader to listen, and "hear" with new ears. Even if that "hearing" is slightly unfamiliar and bold.

It is easy for me to say that Bill is a winsome and erudite author. (Bill and I first collaborated many years ago when he wrote one of the most imaginative and dramatic biographies of C. S. Lewis ever published).* Bill's deep reverence for this literature imbues his paraphrase with a magnanimous spirit.

---

*William Griffin, *Clive Staples Lewis: A Dramatic Life*, originally published by HarperSanFrancisco, 1986, reissued by Lion/Hudson, 2006.

I am proud to be a part of this venture and to be able to lend my publishing support to these volumes. One final note. Even though these words were written hundreds of years ago in a different time and place they truly are a treasure.

Roy M. Carlisle
Senior Editor

Of Related Interest

THOMAS A KEMPIS
CONSOLATIONS FOR MY SOUL
translated by William Griffin

A hidden classic!
First English translation in four hundred years!

Such consolations as the book offers were meant to help the soul
weather the storm and stress found in every healthy spiritual life.
Indeed the word "consolation" as used by Kempis is just another
word for grace. As such it's the lubricant for the soul, the engine
that has no parts. The more the consolations or graces, the fewer
the squeaks as the soul wend its weary way to its own true home.

"There is so much helpful counsel from the old writers that most
of us know nothing of. Thank you for bringing this piece to us."

— RICHARD FOSTER, author *of Celebration of Discipline,*
Prayer — The Heart's True Home, and a dozen other books;
founder of RENOVARE

"As always, whatever springs from your pen and keyboard makes
for good reading and lifting of the spirit."

— LUCI SHAW, author of *Water My Soul* and *The Angles of Light*;
Writer in Residence, Regent College, Vancouver

"I've just received it, and I'm already consoled by my reading of it.
It is surely the world's Most Beautiful Paperback.

— WALTER HOOPER, literary adviser to the estate of C. S. Lewis

"It was sheer pleasure, listening to your natural, playful rendering."

— CHRISTOPHER WEBB, Renewal Officer,
Council for Ministry, The Church in Wales

ISBN 0-8245-2107-2, paperback, $19.95

crossroad

Of Related Interest

Karen Kuchan, Ph.D.
VISIO DIVINA
A New Practice of Prayer for Healing and Growth

A remarkable new development in Christian prayer!

Join others today who are finding God's healing, forgiveness, and love through Visio Divina. In *Visio Divina,* meditative and healing prayer is used with a particular image that God reveals for the discovery of hidden wounds and desires. Dr. Kuchan weaves together practical explanations of this new practice, along with stories of people who have used it to overcome shame and anger as they discover divine acceptance and love.

Karen Kuchan, Ph.D., is the founder and president of the Incarnation Center for Spiritual Growth and an adjunct professor at Fuller Seminary in Pasadena, California.

0-8245-2317-2, $16.95 paperback

Please support your local bookstore,
or call 1-800-707-0670 for Customer Service.

For a free catalog, write us at

THE CROSSROAD PUBLISHING COMPANY
481 Eighth Avenue, Suite 1550
New York, NY 10001

Visit our website at
www.crossroadpublishing.com
All prices subject to change.

crossroad